The Lucy Ring

The Lucy Ring

PIERRE ACCOCE

AND

PIERRE QUET

Translated by A. M. Sheridan Smith from the French
La Guerre a été gagnée en Suisse

W. H. ALLEN
LONDON
1967

Illustrations appear between pages 96–97 and 128–129

© Librairie Académique Perrin, 1966
English translation © 1967 by W. H. Allen & Company and
Coward-McCann, Inc.
First British edition, 1967
First impression, January 1967
Second impression, June 1967
Printed and bound in Great Britain by The Garden City Press Limited,
Letchworth, Hertfordshire, for the publishers W. H. Allen & Company,
Essex Street, London WC2

The Lucy Ring

'—the Soviets developed a fantastic source located in Switzerland, a certain Rudolf Roessler (code name "Lucy"). By means which have not been ascertained to this day, Roessler in Switzerland was able to get intelligence from the German High Command in Berlin on a continuous basis, often less than twenty-four hours after its daily decisions concerning the Eastern front were made'—from *The Craft of Intelligence* by Allen Dulles.

1

TUESDAY, SEPTEMBER 8, 1942.
The Swiss customs post at the entrance to the international
bridge at Laufenburg, on the Rhine, had been alerted. The
day before, the federal authorities at Lucerne had announced
that a special civilian would cross the bridge into Germany.
He was to be neither searched nor questioned. Moreover,
he would have no identity papers. The time was fixed for
8.15 a.m.

On that clear summer morning, war seemed very far
away. Yet the battle continued to rage before Stalingrad,
where the resistance of the Russians grew tougher every
day. In North Africa, the Royal Air Force was helping to
halt the advance of Rommel's tanks.

The Rhine cuts Laufenburg in two, but the two halves
of the town are very similar in character. The houses that
rise up on both sides of the valley were all built about the
same time; for three centuries these buildings have faced
each other across the river. The narrow, winding streets on
the German and Swiss sides are paved with the same
cobblestones. The granite bridge that links them together

7

is forty metres long and five metres wide and has two arches. In the middle, a small turret flanked by two shrubs protrudes over the grey, fast-moving river. On the Swiss side is an esplanade, the Laufenplatz, planted with alder-trees and adorned by an octagonal fountain dating from 1763. Near this monument, in a shed protected with sand-bags, a platoon of territorial guards were garrisoned. Since the outbreak of war, these troops had provided reinforcements at the various customs posts along the frontiers. The two entrances to the Laufenplatz—the Laufengasse and the Fischergasse—had been blocked by barricades and barbed wire. On the German side there were also sand-bags and barbed wire. A large, three-storeyed building with a dark tiled roof seemed to block the entrance to the bridge: this was an inn, the Gasthof Laufen.

The guard on the German side had also been warned, from Berlin, to expect the unusual civilian. He was to be conducted as far as the Gasthof Laufen. Then a counter-order arrived—he was to be taken straight to the post on the right side of the bridge. The guard knew no more than that, but he was a little concerned about the man sitting in the post sipping coffee, and who had arrived to receive the civilian. He was obviously a member of the Gestapo.

At exactly 8.15 a.m., a black car moved up the Fischergasse and stopped near the Swiss customs post, just in front of the Gasthaus zum Meerfräulein, an inn famous throughout the north of Switzerland: at the front of the hotel a sign depicts a woman with large, bare breasts. Two men got out of the car: a captain of the Swiss Federal Army, in grey-green uniform, and the mysterious civilian. The customs officers checked their positions and without a word opened the barricade. The captain went through first, followed by the civilian. With short, hurried steps he crossed the esplanade in the direction of the bridge. At this point, a sergeant of the territorials ran out of the shed near the fountain. "Halt! The civilian can't go through."

On the other side of the bridge, the German customs officer looked up.

The civilian turned to the captain and growled: "They forgot to warn the territorials. You'd better sort it out, Meyer. I've got to get through."

The captain tried to explain, but the sergeant was adamant.

"I can't agree to it, sir. You know my orders. No one is to go through without a special visa."

The officer insisted.

"I'm very sorry, sir," interrupted the sergeant. "There's only one man in the whole of Switzerland who could give me orders to let anyone through without a visa. And that's Brigadier Masson!"

A bitter argument ensued. The captain got his way only after signing a discharge, freeing the territorials from all responsibility for contravening the regulations. As the civilian stepped on to the bridge, the captain stood to attention and saluted.

The civilian was trembling as he walked towards Germany. It was a narrow escape. It could have led to a major scandal. But his incognito had been preserved. He believed he had thought of everything to make his crossing as speedy and inconspicuous as possible, and the recent incident had been a silly oversight: he should have remembered that. After all, they were his own orders, for this 'civilian' was none other than Brigadier Masson himself, the head of the entire Swiss information and counter-espionage services. There he was, the 'boss' himself, who had under his command some 300,000 police, frontier guards, customs guards and secret agents, setting out on a mission. It was to be one of the strangest and most decisive missions in his career.

The German customs officer observed him with curiosity. Since August 30, 1939, few people had crossed the bridge, most of them local inhabitants. What was this small, nervous man, sucking an old pipe, doing crossing into Germany with all its restrictions?

"They're expecting me," said the civilian.

The customs officer said nothing. He raised the barrier,

stepped back, opened the office door and, when the civilian entered, quickly shut it behind him. Masson looked surprised, for the man in the light green raincoat sitting at the table was not the man he expected to meet. This looked very like the Gestapo.

The stranger got up from the table. "I'm afraid there's been a slight hitch, monsieur. Er, to whom have I the honour . . .? Ah, you prefer not to reveal yourself. As you wish. You were expecting General Schellenberg, I believe? The general won't be coming. Not here, anyway. He's had a car accident. Oh, nothing serious. Nothing to worry about. Major Eggen, his aide, has telephoned to say that he will come and collect you within a couple of hours. Have you met Eggen?"

Masson knew a great deal about H. W. Eggen. As well as being an SS man—Sturmbannführer, and Schellenberg's secretary, he had an important post with a large industrial group in Berlin, the Warenvertrieb GMBH. A curious situation! Eggen also had considerable financial interests in Lausanne. When given the job of supplying the Wehrmacht with huts, he placed the order in Switzerland. He had been dealing with two representatives of the Swiss timber industry—Paul Holzach and P. Meyer, alias Schwertenbach—since November 1940. This P. Meyer was none other than the man who had just accompanied Masson to the frontier. For these two businessmen, mobilised into the Swiss forces as captains, were Masson's aides. Eggen was not unaware of this—and it was the reason, apart from the timber, why he cultivated them so assiduously, meeting them almost every month at the Interkommertz A.G. in Zürich.

Masson trusted Holzach and Meyer completely—especially Meyer, who had already served under him when the future head of Swiss Intelligence commanded the artillery section of the 1st Division. At the repeated request of Eggen, Meyer decided to introduce the German to Roger Masson. The meeting took place on Wednesday, December 10, 1941, during one of the SS-Sturmbannführer's many business visits. The meeting was cordial enough. The two men discussed the relations between Switzerland and the Third Reich. Masson complained of the virulence of the attacks on his country in the German press. Eggen expressed the view that this problem could certainly be resolved to Masson's satisfaction, and suggested that the brigadier should be put into contact with Eggen's friend, superior and 'spiritual master', SS-Brigadeführer Schellenberg, who had influence in the highest quarters. Masson did not regard such a meeting as being very urgent and declined to take up the offer at once. He did not, at that time, imagine that less than a year later events would force him to ask Major Eggen to arrange a meeting with Schellenberg!

The unknown German at the customs post of Klein-Laufenburg—or little Laufenburg, the name given to the German township to distinguish it from the Swiss Laufenburg—plied Masson with questions. He was astonished that Masson could cross the frontier so easily. Who was he? What did the Swiss think of the way the war was going? Did they have any doubts as to the ultimate victory of National Socialism?

It was a difficult situation. With increasing anxiety, Masson gradually revealed himself. What was happening? And what about this car accident that could compromise everything? There he was, the head of Swiss Intelligence, trapped in Germany, in the hands of the worst elements in the Nazi régime. Masson was perfectly well aware of the feelings of the Nazi leaders towards him. The Reichsführer SS Heinrich Himmler, for example, had been known to shout during one of his famous fits of anger, when he would fire off pistol-shots in his office: "I pay whoever gives me service; he who gives me disservice pays. I have no enemies. If I do make any, then I liquidate them. The scum of the earth will be liquidated, including Churchill and Roosevelt—and Masson, that Swiss who has sided with them ever since war broke out!"

At 10.30 a relaxed, affable Sturmbannführer H. W. Eggen arrived. Yes, on the road from Berlin to Klein-Laufenburg,

General Schellenberg's Mercedes crashed into a ditch. They were saved by a miracle. The general sent his apologies for the delay. They had been forced to come by train. But the meeting could still take place—but not at Klein-Laufenburg. They would go to Waldshut, fifteen kilometres up the Rhine, to the Station Hotel.

Fifteen winding, twisting kilometres along the banks of the river. The major, it seemed, was driving a vehicle that had been requisitioned at Waldshut.

Roger Masson had reason to feel apprehensive. Should he believe Eggen? After all, Schellenberg could quite easily have come to Laufenburg—with Eggen, or by train. Why had he chosen Waldshut? Had he been trying to sap Masson's morale by inflicting on him that agonising wait with the Gestapo officer? Was it all part of the technique of secret warfare? The thirty-two year old SS-Brigadeführer, also head of the Sicherheitsdienst, the German Political Intelligence Service, was just the man to think up such a ruse. He had a reputation for just such action.

On the evening of November 8, 1939, for example, in a restaurant in Munich, where every year Hitler celebrated the anniversary of his failed putsch of 1923, there was an attempt on the Führer's life. Suddenly Hitler broke off his speech and fled from the table, just before a bomb clumsily concealed in a pillar, exploded. He was to recount later how a voice within had urged him to leave. But everything had led political and technical observers to believe that the whole thing had been pre-arranged by the Nazis themselves in an attempt to increase the Führer's popularity.

In the early hours of the morning of November 9, Walter Schellenberg went into action. At Venlo, in Holland, very close to the German frontier, he led a group of SS and arrested two British officers: Captain Best and Major Stevens, British Intelligence agents. Since October 21, he had accused the two officers of working for a group of German generals who wished to overthrow Hitler and set up a new régime with the blessing of Great Britain. In fact, he was holding them in readiness for the right moment.

Captain Best and Major Stevens, accused of having organised the Munich plot from Venlo, were to spend the rest of the war in a concentration camp. This accusation was also to serve, shortly afterwards, as a pretext for the invasion of Holland—such an attack being justified on the grounds that 'this country has abused the privileges of neutrality by harbouring two such violent enemies of the Third Reich.'

Hitler was delighted by the success of this ruse. It led him to give Schellenberg the job of working out, and carrying out personally, a plan to kidnap the Duke and Duchess of Windsor. The Führer believed that he could persuade the ex-King of England to collaborate with him and arrange a peace with Britain. At the end of July 1940, the royal couple were in Lisbon. They were to be given a residence in Germany, and some £40,000—already placed in a bank in Geneva—was to be put at their disposal. If necessary, Hitler would increase the amount. The kidnapping failed by a hair's breadth, for British Intelligence agents arrived in Portugal one day before the young SS general.

Masson was able to complete his picture of Walter Schellenberg by his own sources of information. German anti-Nazi circles in Switzerland described him as a 'gentleman assassin' who was capable of anything. 'A man with a particularly open, frank expression, charming and well-mannered, but, in fact, a real gangster' was how Walter Schellenberg was described by Hans Bernd Gisevius, German Vice-Consul and one of Hitler's leading opponents, and the organiser of the attempt on Hitler's life on July 20, 1944.

Walter Schellenberg was a kind of Nazi 'intellectual' and talked brilliantly of music, literature and painting. He claimed to despise politics—yet, at thirty-two, he was the youngest of the Nazi leaders, the man whom Himmler affectionately called his 'Benjamin'. Of all Hitler's generals he was the most widely travelled. But he never left his headquarters in the Berkaerstrasse, in Berlin-Schmargendorf, without good reason. It was from there that he ran the 'F' bureaux of the Sicherheitsdienst, that is, all his espionage networks throughout the world.

Brigadier Roger Masson had gone into Germany in order to save one of his men. But he was now panic-stricken, for he knew that he was caught in one of the SS Brigadeführer's Machiavellian traps. He could even end up in Schellenberg's triumphant grasp, as Best and Stevens—or worse, perhaps.

It was a clever trap, brought about by a mistake made by one of his less experienced assistants. Two months before, in July 1942, Masson had appointed a certain young Lieutenant Möergeli as a clerk in the Swiss consulate in Stuttgart. Möergeli quietly carried out a minor mission. He supplied a certain amount of information concerning the movements of the Wehrmacht in the areas adjoining the Swiss frontier.

One evening, in a brasserie, the Swiss lieutenant made the acquaintance of a German civilian, who soon declared himself to be a staunch anti-Nazi. Möergeli was imprudent enough to express approval, thus falling into a trap of infantile simplicity. The Swiss officer was immediately arrested and condemned to death. The consul informed Berne, which passed the message on to Masson in Lucerne, asking him if he could intervene.

Masson realised that there was some significance in the disproportion between Möergeli's error and the punishment with which he was threatened. It was clear that the Sicherheitsdienst, which had provoked the whole episode, wanted to contact Masson himself. Moreover, they intended to put him into a position of inferiority from the beginning. Masson would be forced to ask for a favour. But what would Schellenberg want in return?

The car driven by Eggen entered Waldshut—an old tourist town of 10,000 inhabitants, built on a hill overlooking the Rhine. The road ran beside the railway. Just before the station, they turned right along the Poststrasse. The Bahnhof Hotel was a grey, gloomy, three-storeyed building. Major Eggen led Masson to a small, dark oak-panelled lounge, where the walls were adorned with hunting trophies—boars' heads and deer-antlers, reminding one that the Black Forest was not far away.

Eggen went out. Shortly afterwards a man pushed open the door. He was tall and slim—perhaps six feet tall—and was wearing a superbly cut grey tweed suit. His thick, brown hair was combed straight back and parted on the left. He had a wide sensual mouth, gentle, deep-set eyes and an attractive smile. Masson had no difficulty in recognising Walter Schellenberg. He was exactly like the photographs his Lucerne office had supplied him with before his departure. His voice, too, was gentle, with a slight touch of irony in its tone.

"I dare say you're thinking that this hotel is filled with cameras and microphones, Monsieur Masson. After all, it's what you'd expect in wartime, don't you think? I suggest we go outside. We can sit on whichever bench you choose along the embankment by the Rhine."

The two men walked down the Poststrasse and turned right into the Bismarkstrasse. Fifteen yards ahead, on the left, was a path which led to the embankment, the Rheinweg. Here, too, there were alders overhanging the river. The broad walk was deserted. A few seats faced the river. On the other side, in the distance, was Switzerland, hidden behind a light mist.

Schellenberg attacked at once. "I must warn you at the outset, Monsieur Masson, that I came here only after a great deal of hesitation. I have reason to believe that your intelligence service is in the pay of the Americans. And here's my proof."

The SS general held out a paper. Masson read it through quickly. It was a copy of a cable sent by the American military attaché in Berne to Washington in 1940.

In June of that year, Masson had called a meeting of foreign military attachés. It was feared that Switzerland was about to be invaded. Panic was sweeping through northern Switzerland, emptying its towns and villages. Every room, every bed had been taken along the banks of Lake Geneva. The American military attaché asked if it was true that there were twenty-five German divisions stationed between Basle and Lake Constance. Masson had just received secret reports on the subject. Between Basle and Karlsruhe there were no more than four divisions: the 554th, the 555th, the 556th and the 557th. Under cover in the Black Forest, south of Ulm and Rastatt, were five more, fully equipped. This was not enough to invade Switzerland. Careful to observe the strictest neutrality, Masson replied that 'there was a lot going off' to the north of Switzerland.

Impressed by the importance of this information and anxious to emphasise his own part in the matter, the American military attaché immediately sent off a cable to Washington: 'Extraordinary meeting with Masson. He confirmed to me that there are twenty-five German divisions near the Swiss frontier. He added that they are ready to attack.'

He then gave the cable to a courier from his embassy to take to the experts for coding. This courier was a German agent. He copied out the text of the message and sent it off to Berlin. It was this copy that, two years later, Schellenberg showed to Masson.

Masson handed the paper back.

"This does not prove that Washington finances my services. And you know it, Brigadeführer. Perhaps you wanted to show me how efficient your espionage service could be? But I don't need to be shown that, General."

Schellenberg's face lit up with a curious smile. "What do you want from me, Monsieur Masson."

"That, too, you know. I asked for this meeting—with the agreement of my superior, General Guisan. Only he and Colonel Barbey, his private chief of staff, know I am here. This is an official visit as their representative to show that our position is frequently misunderstood in Germany, and that we are determined to defend ourselves against any aggressor. I have also come to ask you to give up the intensive espionage system you are now building up against us."

Masson paused for a moment, then, carefully choosing his words, he went on: "I would also like you to know that I am no fool. I admit I have been forced to come here to ask for the pardon and safe return of Lieutenant Möergeli, one of my officers in Stuttgart, who was arrested by your services."

Schellenberg showed no hesitation: "Agreed."

The brevity of the reply and the ease with which the general acceded to the request surprised Masson. Now, what will the Brigadeführer want in exchange?

"Have you no other request, Monsieur Masson?"

Was Schellenberg making fun of him? And what did he want? Since 1941, two Swiss Nazis, Ernst Leonhardt and Franz Burri, had settled in Vienna and set up an agency, the International Press Agentur. They were conducting a violent campaign against the Confederation, attacking Guisan and the principles of Swiss neutrality. Many of their publications were getting into Switzerland via Lörrach and Basle.

"Have you heard of the *International Press Agentur*, General Schellenberg? Its vicious attacks on our country are a great embarrassment to us. Could you stop this source of distorted information?"

"Agreed."

Schellenberg rose and turned to Masson.

"I speak for the Reich when I say that we should not like the relations between our two countries to be disturbed in any way. Switzerland is a neutral country and should remain as such. A world at war needs somewhere where it can breathe freely. That place could be Switzerland. Within a month you will have Möergeli back, and the agency run by Burri and Leonhardt will cease its attacks.

"But I must warn you that in Berlin, in Ribbentrop's office in the Ministry of Foreign Affairs, there is a very incriminating 'Masson file', containing a great deal of information supplied by Burri and Leonhardt. I shall try and get hold of it. There's a lot I can do, you know. By the way! The chief of your police division, Rothmund . . . thanks to me, he will get his visa to go to Berlin to settle some business about secret frontier crossings. He will get it within the next twenty-four hours. . . . Let us go back to the Bahnhof for a little refreshment. They have some Dole. I know you're very fond of this wine. Sturmbannführer

Eggen will then take you to the bridge at Koblentz. It's no more than two kilometres away. I dare say you would like to get back to Switzerland as soon as possible."

The first round of the secret struggle between Germany and Switzerland seemed to have been entirely to Masson's advantage. Without argument, and without in the least committing himself, he had obtained everything he wanted. And Schellenberg had asked for nothing.

In fact, Schellenberg's amazing amiability on the occasion of that meeting was no more than yet another example of his diabolical cunning. While secretly forcing his hand, he had left it to Masson to make the first contact. If that meeting at Waldshut, and the others that followed, were to become known one day, it would be the head of Swiss Intelligence who would be criticised. If the Allies learnt of these meetings Switzerland would be suspected of a tendency to *rapprochement* that was contrary to her own will and interests. One may well wonder if, apart from the many qualities that made Walter Schellenberg one of the most remarkable secret agents of the last war, he did not also have to an unusual degree the ability to anticipate the future.

The foresight that he showed on that occasion was even more far-reaching. By granting a pardon to Möergeli and by promising to close down the *International Press Agentur*, he had quite simply put the Swiss in his debt—and without revealing earlier than he wished his motives for doing so. He now knew that entry to the last island of free territory, encircled in a Europe that was going up in flames, would not now be entirely denied him. He had forced a way in and this would help him to succeed in a very difficult task. At least, so he hoped. In fact, he was looking for something in Switzerland, something of inestimable value for Germany, for on it depended the very survival of the Third Reich.

2

ERMATINGEN IS A BIG VILLAGE
on the edge of Lake Constance. To the right of the small
village square is an inn at which, it is said, Napoleon spent
a night during his conquest of Europe. A narrow road
winds its way up the hill-side into a thick forest, where
there are herds of deer. It leads to Sonterswil. But before it
reaches Sonterswil, at a distance of about one-and-a-half
kilometres from Ermatingen, it emerges on to a plateau. In
the middle of this clearing is a large sixteenth-century
building, known, rather pompously, as a *schloss*. In fact, it
is more like a manor house than a castle. Its windows provide a magnificent view over the lake. This is Wolfsberg,
then the home of Captain Meyer, also known as Schwertenbach, one of Masson's aides.

It was here, on the morning of Friday, October 16, 1942,
that General Walter Schellenberg and the head of Swiss
Intelligence met for the second time. It was arranged, as in
September, on the initiative of the SS officer. A few days
before, his acolyte, SS-Sturmbannführer Eggen, had re-

marked to P. Meyer that "it would be a pity not to take advantage of the growing mutual understanding between the heads of the secret services of the Reich and the Swiss Confederation . . . Schellenberg would very much like to come to Switzerland. . . ."

So with the approval of General Guisan, Brigadier Masson agreed to invite the SS general. A secluded place had to be found for the meeting. Meyer offered the use of his own house—it was on a small, little-used road, well away from any other place of habitation.

It was important that the SS general should pass unnoticed. Swiss public opinion was now violently anti-German. This had largely been brought about by Gauleiter Böhle, whose special responsibility was the care of Nazi organisations outside Germany. On October 4, 1942, he left Germany to preside at a harvest festival meeting in the Hallenstadion in Zürich. In fact, it was a large-scale Nazi ceremony, complete with violent speeches and military songs, attended by large numbers of Germans who happened, at that time, to be in Switzerland. This was undoubtedly a tactical error on the part of the Germans. The Swiss were not at all pleased and there were angry manifestations in the streets. The situation was so dangerous that the Federal Council had to forbid all meetings of foreigners on its territory.

What is more, Ermatingen was in the German-speaking part of the country—and the German-speaking Swiss hated Nazism even more than did their French-speaking compatriots. For them, Nazism was a betrayal, the very negation of the German culture that many of them had received in German universities. In the event of invasion, they too would be in the front lines—and they were well aware that the Brown Shirts would like to take over their country. Maps had been distributed by Nazi propagandists that left no doubt as to the Führer's intentions. These maps, showing the Europe of the future and the frontiers of the Great Reich, destined to endure for a thousand years, quite clearly enclosed the whole of German-speaking Switzerland.

If any doubt remained, one only had to read the German press which was filled with attacks on the Confederation. The Swiss responded so violently in their own newspapers that Brigadier Masson began to fear the worst.

He learnt that Ribbentrop's men were compiling dossiers on German-speaking Swiss journalists, collecting irrefutable proof of their hostility to Germany. Messages had already been received from Berlin demanding that the editors of the three most important papers in the Confederation should be sacked, and that the head of the *Agence Télégraphique Suisse* should be severely reprimanded for the partiality of his radio communiqués. When these suggestions were not taken up, the head of the press section in the Foreign Ministry publicly threatened the journalists from Berlin: after the occupation of Switzerland they would be sent to the Russian steppes and even farther east. This tactic came to be known as the *Blutschuldthese*—the thesis that if blood flowed in Switzerland, then it would be entirely the fault of the Swiss press.

Brigadier Masson was in favour of more subtle action through diplomatic channels, and regarded his countrymen's behaviour as childish. He had tried in vain to appease this overt hatred of the Germans. At last, he burst out angrily: "If they really want to let themselves go, why don't they come out openly on the side of the Allies and fight the Germans!"

However, Masson had no desire to exacerbate an already explosive situation and arranged for his meeting with Schellenberg to take place in the greatest secrecy. At dawn on Friday, October 16, 1942, Masson's chauffeur, Renaud, collected Schellenberg and Eggen—wearing civilian clothes, of course—at the frontier, without anyone suspecting their identity. At Wolfsberg, besides Masson and Meyer, was Captain Paul Holzach. They welcomed the SS officers warmly. The Germans would stay until the Sunday evening. Despite the warm, sunny autumn weather, they would not leave the house. No risks must be taken. And no expense would be spared to make this long weekend as pleasant as possible for their guests. Masson was hoping for a great deal from this meeting.

In the course of these three days, Walter Schellenberg was at his most charming. He amused his hosts with juggling, card-tricks and conjuring-tricks. After a particularly good dinner, as they sat in front of the log fire in the great drawing-room, the SS-Brigadeführer became more expansive.

He was born in the Saar in 1910, the youngest of seven children—he was old enough to remember the horrors of the First World War. He was seven then and living at Saarbrück when he experienced his first air-raid—the French were bombing his city. He would never forget the cold, the hunger and the misery of that terrible winter.

His father was a piano-maker—not a very propitious trade in 1923, when an exhausted, impoverished Germany thought more of appeasing its hunger than of amusing itself. So the family emigrated to Luxembourg. In the summer of 1929, Walter went to Bonn University. For two years he studied medicine, then took up law. The world crisis and the desperate economic situation in Germany, which was not helped by the degenerating political atmosphere of the Weimar Republic, did not leave the Schellenbergs unaffected. The student was forced to ask for a scholarship to complete his studies. The judge who was dealing with his case hinted that he would have more chance of obtaining this help if he joined the Nazi party and the SS organisation. Suddenly, everything appeared to be quite simple.

One day, in 1934, Schellenberg gave a lecture on the development of German law, in the course of which he made an attack on the Catholic Church. This attracted the attention of Reinhard Heydrich, head of the Sicherheitsdienst until his death on June 4, 1942. Two of Heydrich's advisors, both professors at Bonn University, approached Schellenberg and engaged him. Yes, the future certainly looked bright. But he owed his extraordinary success to his own gifts, to hard work—not to favouritism, so rampant in

Germany since the Nazis had come to power. If, since Heydrich's death, Himmler had taken him into his confidence, it was because of his ability as a jurist and because of his profound knowledge of western Europe. The Reichsführer had even ordered his own doctor, a Finn called Karsten, who was utterly devoted to him, to take particular care of Schellenberg's health—he suffered from a bad liver.

He was also on very close terms with Admiral Canaris. Every morning, when they were both in Berlin, they went riding together. In the open air they are able to exchange confidential information without danger of eavesdroppers. The head of the Abwehrstelle was something less than careful in his choice of assistants. He tended to swell the ranks of his organisation somewhat indiscriminately. So much so that since 1941, one of Schellenberg's tasks had been the liquidation of certain unreliable elements in the Abwehrstelle. For example, ever since Rommel's Afrika Korps had been fighting on the other side of the Mediterranean, there was not a single oil-tanker, a single troopship or a single German plane whose position was not known in advance by the Allies. If he wasn't more careful, things would turn out very badly indeed for the little admiral.

But to hear him speak, one would imagine that the only thing which mattered, really mattered, to Walter Schellenberg was Irene, his second wife since 1940, who was of Polish descent, and the five children from his first marriage. For someone overwhelmed with work, it was a pleasure to be able to escape from it all for a few days and to come to Switzerland, among friends. He would never forget that weekend.

He needed rest, Schellenberg went on. In Berlin, in the Führer's *entourage*, he was known as a *Märzveilchen*, March violet, a term used to denote those who had rallied to Nazism after the party came to power in March 1933. A lot of people were jealous of him and made things difficult for him. It was an exhausting business being continually on the defensive. The envious could soon be turned into enemies.

Nothing was impossible in that slightly mad, plot-infested Reich of theirs.

"So my office has to be a fortress," he went on. "It is a large room, with a thick carpet. In it there is a very beautiful, old cupboard. I call it my poison-cupboard. In it are my personal files—a habit I picked up from Heydrich. It was he who gave me the most confidential file of all, in which it is proved that Adolf Hitler is of Jewish descent, incredible as that may sound . . . Poor Heydrich! He was obsessed by it—he tried to find Jewish ancestors for everyone around him! On the left of my office is a table, covered with telephones and microphones—my contact with the Chancellery and other services. One of these telephones provides me with a direct line to my Berlin flat, and to my country house in the Herzberg.

"I had to set up a system of photo-electric cells that give the alarm as soon as anyone approaches the chests or my cupboard in my absence. When I'm there, two machine-guns concealed in my desk are trained on whoever is talking to me. In an emergency, I simply press a button. . . .

"When I go abroad on a mission, I have an artificial tooth fixed. It contains a dose of poison that could kill me if ever I fell into the hands of the Allies. . . !

To prove his point, Schellenberg opened his mouth and showed Masson his tooth. With a slight smile, he took out the large blue stone from the ring he was wearing. In the bezel was a small transparent capsule containing cyanide.

Had the SS general come to Switzerland simply to talk about himself, then? Or for a rest? He had not mentioned his previous meeting with Masson. Yet he had kept his word—the *International Press Agentur* had suddenly stopped the flood into Switzerland of its tendentious publications; and Möergeli, the young lieutenant condemned to death in Stuttgart, had been freed. A plane had taken him to the military airfield at Dübendorf, near Zürich, where his fiancée, tipped off by the secret service in Lucerne, was awaiting him.

Meyer, Holzach and Major Eggen often wandered off to

discuss timber and other business matters. The SS-Sturm-bannführer promised Meyer, whom he knew to be a good horseman, a fine chestnut bay, as well as an Old Master, in recognition of his good offices and hospitality.

Masson and Schellenberg spoke of the war, and of the miseries that it entailed. The German general emphasised how desirable and reasonable it would be to sign a compromise peace with the West; by agreeing to return, in Europe, to the frontiers of September 1939, the whole weight of the Wehrmacht could then be thrown against Bolshevism in the East. Britain was still too weak to open a second front and was awaiting the arrival of strategic materials from America. This aid was slow in coming. When the United States threw in their full strength, the balance would be destroyed, to the detriment of Germany.

Schellenberg mentioned that he had discussed this problem with Himmler two months earlier, in August 1942, at Jitomir on the Russian front. He had even suggested to the Reichsführer that the constitution of the new Europe that could be created should be based on that of Switzerland, which was a perfect model. He had added that the Confederation formed a link between Germany and the West, as well as an office for settling matters of trade and currency. Himmler had agreed that he should try and make approaches to the West. And he undertook to convince Hitler before Christmas 1942—and at the same time to eliminate Ribbentrop, who was implacably opposed to any idea of a separate peace. He cuts a poor figure as a Foreign Minister, don't you think? An ex-champagne dealer, nicknamed Ribbensnob, the lover of Edda Ciano, the Duce's daughter. . . .

Brigadier Masson was interested, but also infuriated by this gossip. For Schellenberg had said nothing about the real problem, nor thrown any light on why he had come to Switzerland. If he wanted to meet the British, nothing could be easier! Berne was at their disposal.

In fact, Schellenberg was already doing that. He had long ago sent his most trusted agent, Jahnke, to Berne.

Jahnke was a giant of a man from Pomerania, extremely clever, and one of the best spies in the German secret service of pre-Hitler days. In 1935, he became Rudolf Hess's information expert. Schellenberg had used him because he knew Chiang Kai-Shek and other important Chinese families very well—and because he also had useful contacts in Japan.

When he was living in the United States, from 1920, he set up a service for the transfer of dead bodies. He transported to China all the 'Sons of Heaven' who had died in America, it being part of their religion that they should be buried in their homeland. A thousand dollars per coffin! This work and the contacts that it had produced had made Jahnke the German specialist in Far Eastern affairs. And it was as such that he had been sent by Schellenberg to Berne, the main centre of the Asian secret services. But his real work was to make contact with the British, to persuade them that there were men around the Führer with whom they could talk, that they were not all fanatics.

The night of October 18 arrived and Schellenberg had still not revealed his intentions. Masson was hesitant about broaching the subject. It would soon be time for the two SS officers to return to Germany. At last, the brigadier made up his mind. In the most relaxed way possible, he mentioned the existence of a document that could be very compromising for Switzerland. . . .

It concerned a decision made by General Guisan with the assent of the political bureau of the Federal Council, but which could have severe consequences for the future of the Confederation. It could partly justify the permanent accusation levelled against Switzerland by Germany that it should no longer be regarded as a neutral country. Switzerland had, in fact, chosen the side of the Allies, well before the Wehrmacht had invaded Europe. Henri Guisan had signed a secret agreement with General Gamelin, with France. It was a military convention whereby the Confederation could ask for the help of French troops, and even allow them access to their territory, if their strategic needs so required it.

It was an explosive document that should never have got into the hands of the Germans.

But this information had got into their hands, as Masson had known for some time, He had received proof of this shortly before meeting Walter Schellenberg at Waldshut—and in a very curious way.

The affair began in 1940. After the appointment of General Weygand as chief of the French Army, General Maurice Gamelin abandoned a train that was carrying the archives of General Headquarters at Charité-sur-Loire. On June 19, German troops discovered the train and alerted Major-General Ulrich Liss, head of the 3rd section of the G.Ic, one of the secret services of the Wehrmacht.

Liss had the convoy thoroughly searched. The booty was of astonishing proportions: whole cases filled with confidential documents. For example, the text of an agreement of co-operation between the French and Belgian armies, dated November 9, 1939; the details of the cover given to the troops on the Escaut, dated November 15, 1939; the plan of action and the identities of the French special agents in Rumania, directed by Léon Wenger, of the Pétrofina company, whose mission was the destruction of the petroleum plants supplying the Reich; the codes used by the Allies; a top-secret note concerning the conduct of the war and, in particular, the attitude to be observed towards neutrals aiding Germany, meaning, at that stage, Sweden.

"At the moment," noted Major-General Liss, who studied all the documents, "the information contained in this convoy is of little more than historical value. . . . Except, that is, for an interesting French military convention with Switzerland!"

And Liss underlined two passages in the treaty:

"On April 14, 1940, General George, commander of the northern front, asked General Gamelin to form a group of nine divisions, which would co-operate with Switzerland."

"On May 20, 1940, General Prételat referred to the task force formed by the 13th and 27th Infantry Divisions, and the 2nd Brigade of Spahis of the 7th Corps of the 8th Army, ordered to make contact with the left flank of the Swiss Army, near Basle, in the Gempen Gap."

If Hitler got to know about these papers, there was no doubt that he would make an official denunciation of Switzerland for violation of its neutrality, and draw military conclusions from the fact. He invaded Holland for less. He attacked Poland on a slender pretext forged by his own secret service.

Having had full knowledge since 1940 of the affair of General Gamelin's train, Brigadier Masson had been wondering anxiously ever since where the terrible document could be. One day in June 1942, Theo Kordt, a counsellor at the German embassy in Berne, with whom he was on friendly terms, confided to him that he had been warned by von Weizaker, Secretary of State of the Third Reich, that the military convention was in the hands of the Sicherheitsdienst in Berlin and could be brandished at any time. The Confederation, therefore, was in grave danger.

Masson had long sought in vain for a means of disconnecting this mine that lay beneath his country's freedom. Then enigmatic Schellenberg arrived on the scene, so mysteriously accommodating. He had certainly got Switzerland in his clutches with the Möergeli affair. He must be expecting something pretty big in return. How could he reply without knowing what exactly his adversary had in mind? How could he catch the German off his guard and get him to reveal what he hoped to do with the convention? Masson therefore assumed a certain frankness with the SS-Brigadeführer.

"You claim to be a friend of Switzerland," he said coaxingly. "Then show it! What do you hope to do with that old treaty now?"

Walter Schellenberg showed no trace of surprise. He knew all about this interesting military convention. He had it in his 'Switzerland' file. He could well understand that the Swiss General should feel uneasy about it. And in order to convince Masson that he was indeed a friend of Switzerland's, he would promise to destroy these papers on his return to Berlin. Berne would never hear of them again.

Would Masson at last learn what Schellenberg wanted in exchange? Masson waited. Nothing.

As he finally took leave of his host, Schellenberg said simply: "I am very concerned for the safety of the Führer."

Only then did Masson realise that Schellenberg had repeated these few words several times during those three days: "I am very concerned for the safety of the Führer."

These words were to haunt Masson during the weeks that followed. He shared his forebodings with General Guisan. Detailed reports had been made of the two meetings he had had with the German officer and sent to the commander-in-chief of the Swiss Army. Masson had written them himself, so that no other person would know of their contents. But with the passing of time, his account of the meetings seemed to take on a disturbing gravity that he had not suspected at the time.

This cunning, manipulating SS general was altogether too elusive. His cautious, cat-like technique of approach showed that he set great store by what he hoped to find in Switzerland. He had tried to embroil Masson in an inextricable net of obligations. He had decided to ask for what he wanted only when he felt that Masson could not refuse him anything. There was still time to get out and Masson told General Guisan quite categorically that he ought to do so. But, while recommending the greatest prudence, the Swiss commander-in-chief insisted on the importance of preserving such a contact.

Towards the close of 1942, Switzerland could not neglect anything that would increase her chances of survival. In general, the situation was not a very hopeful one. Switzerland had shown many signs of sympathy for the Allies. Its anti-aircraft defence, even its fighters, which could be so active and so accurate when it was a question of preventing the Luftwaffe from flying over its territory in 1940, never managed to intercept the thick waves of British bombers as they violated Swiss air space on their way to sow destruction in Germany and northern Italy. It was also a common occurrence, despite the blackout orders announced by the army High Command on November 6, 1940, for Swiss towns to light up 'accidentally' when these planes were passing overhead and thus 'unwittingly' act as guidelights.

Moreover, Switzerland had long been banking secretly on the ultimate victory of the Allies. Despite the supervision exercised by Germany, which had the country completely encircled, Switzerland had continued to send by post to London large quantities of parcels weighing about 4 lb. These contained spare parts for watches, which could also be used for explosive mechanisms.

But these signs still did not satisfy the Allies. The British continued to blockade Switzerland. For some months they had allowed a small number of cargoes to go by sea to Europe and then cross France by train. These cargoes contained goods that were absolutely necessary to Switzerland's survival. Then even this tiny artery was stopped. The Allies criticised the Confederation for continuing to trade with Germany. They refused to admit that she had no other course open to her.

From Germany, Switzerland obtained the coal, iron, mineral oil, petrol, sugar and alcohol that she needed. In exchange, she supplied *Gruyère*, *Emmenthal*, butter and meat, as well as certain industrial products, such as machine-tools and, sometimes, weapon-parts and munitions. It was Walter Krüger, the assistant of the German military attaché in Berne and a man highly trusted by the German Army High Command, who had bought these war materials in Switzerland. So, every day, in every railway-station in the country, secret British supervisors took careful note of everything that left and the destination. Others visited factories and made the most 'intolerable' investigations. Masson's assistants tracked them down, but did nothing to stop their activities.

A British blockade would not really embarrass the Confederation. If there was a shortage of imported corn, the government would ask its farmers to make greater efforts. This was nothing new. On March 8, 1938, an unknown agronomist, F. T. Wahlen, had been appointed by Hermann Obrecht, head of the Department of Public Economy, to work out the potential production of the country's agriculture. Two years later, Wahlen produced the results of his investigations: a detailed plan of action. From the end of 1940, stony ground was cleared, marshes drained and barren land made fertile. Woods were cut down and parks and gardens cleared. Every available piece of ground was sown with seed. Hardy corn, potatoes, beetroots and other vegetables were planted. Colza and poppy were grown for oil. This enormous enterprise was based on an exact calculation of calories and vitamins. It was a complete success. The area of land cultivated rose from 187,000 to 366,000 hectares; the production of potatoes from 80,000 to 180,000 lorry-loads; that of vegetables from 23,000 to 50,000 lorry-loads. But even more could be done.

If the civil mobilisation ordered by F. T. Wahlen to save Switzerland from restrictions made the 'tight belt' policy desired by Britain unnecessary in 1942, and reassured Guisan on this particular score, the Swiss general was very worried on another account. What were the real reasons for the Allies' irritation? The transit across Switzerland of German trains destined for Italy? That, and the loans granted by the Swiss to Germany, and the secret activities of its banks. But there Guisan was helpless. From time to time Germans trying to smuggle money out of the country were expelled —August Schloz and Robert Woter, for example. But these were drops in the ocean.

At the end of the war, the Allies were to claim that the gold stolen by the Germans in Europe and transferred to the safety of secret safes in Switzerland was of the value of about 800 million French francs—1945 francs. On January 5, 1943, through the press, the Allies urged all neutral countries, including Switzerland, not to accept this stolen gold, which at the time totalled something like 585 million dollars worth. This appeal was repeated by the Americans on February 23, 1944. But the Swiss bankers do not appear to have paid any attention.

Belgian gold is not included in this figure of 800 million francs. In 1939, the National Bank of Belgium entrusted part of its gold reserves to the Bank of France, asking for it to be placed in safety. At the end of May 1940, Belgium asked Paris to transfer the gold from Bordeaux to London on a British cruiser, whose commander had already been warned. The French certainly transferred the gold—but on a French ship and to Dakar.

On October 29, 1940, the Bank of France promised to return this gold to Belgium. But Pierre Laval sent it to Berlin, where it was 'requisitioned'. Melted down and supplied with false seals and false papers, the gold was transferred to Switzerland by the Germans. The Swiss National Bank remembered very well having accepted, for 378.6 million Swiss francs, a quantity of gold of unknown origin. Moreover, another consignment of the same gold, equivalent to 153 million Swiss francs was deposited in Berne by the Reichsbank and re-sold to other, unknown parties. In 1945, when France, restoring to Brussels the equivalent of the gold that had been entrusted to her, claimed what had been transferred to Switzerland by the Germans, Berne declared that it held only 160 million francs worth of this treasure in its safes. The difference of 218.6 million Swiss francs had been resold long ago to supply the needs of its banking operations.

So, suspecting, in 1942, that the end of the war could present Switzerland with a number of problems, and feeling no doubt that his country might well be unable to assuage the bitterness that was bound to be shown towards her, Guisan preferred not to lose contact with Schellenberg, who stated quite clearly that he wanted to negotiate with the Allies. If the Brigadeführer succeeded, the Confederation would benefit from the general relaxation of tension. Such a success might even rebound in part to his own credit. The Swiss frontiers would be open for Schellenberg whenever he wanted to come; all that was necessary was for him to be watched closely.

At that time, in its precariously balanced position between

Germany and the Allies, Switzerland could not afford to neglect anything that might be of help. If, in 1942, the Reich showed signs of a general weakening, there was nothing to show that it would necessarily lose the war. Bets therefore had to be made—and it would be as well to spread them as widely as possible. On the other hand, one had to prepare for the future, for an Allied victory, and to continue to give signs of support.

The Swiss frontiers were opened to receive large numbers of men of the French Resistance. There is abundant evidence of the secret and highly effective help that was given daily by the Swiss to those who were fighting against Nazism. Guillain de Bénouville, Michel Hollard, Colonel Groussard, Rémy—to mention only a few of the great names of the Resistance—have told of the indispensable co-operation shown by the Swiss. But in 1942, Switzerland also had to live. At whatever cost to its leaders nothing must be done, nothing could be done that would alarm Germany and provoke her to violent reaction.

In order to understand in all its complexity the tense, difficult, subtle game then being played by Switzerland, none of the cards she had been led to play should be overlooked. When SS Brigadeführer Schellenberg showed a particular interest in Switzerland, it was because he believed that Switzerland was hiding part of her stakes from Germany—her stake in the future—and Switzerland had to make important concessions to the policies of the Reich— her stake in the present. If Hitler had sent Walter Schellenberg to Switzerland in order to win concessions of the greatest importance to the Reich, without having to resort to the ultimate means of persuasion, that is, military intervention, it was because the Swiss leaders had already proved that they could be talked to. Nothing but non-committal conversations and unformulated concessions had been achieved. But this, at least, was something.

On October 18, 1942, when Walter Schellenberg arrived back in Berlin, the war was raging on all fronts and no one could predict the outcome. The Americans had just involved themselves in an uncertain battle at Guadalcanal in the Pacific. Violent, but other uncertain battles were being waged in the industrial districts of Stalingrad. And the night before, an RAF squadron of ninety-four planes had bombed Le Creusot, causing forty dead and eighty wounded. More than ever before, Switzerland had to act with the greatest prudence. There must be no conflict with Germany. Moreover, on October 17, in the presence of Herr Kobelt, chief of the Military Department, the Swiss equivalent of Defence Minister, a football match had taken place at Lausanne at which Germany had beaten Switzerland 5-3—evidence, surely, of the good relations existing between the two countries. Yes, Schellenberg had every reason to feel satisfied. He knew that the contact with Switzerland could not be broken, that the Swiss were well aware of the strength of the Reich and the need to maintain relations with it.

3

"THE MOST UNIVERSAL QUALITY of the human mind is its diversity," wrote Montaigne. This sentence was Walter Schellenberg's favourite maxim. It hung, framed, on the walls of his office, just behind his desk. General Guisan and Brigadier Masson were wondering when he would emerge once more from his lair in Berlin. But he had not forgotten them. He was simply letting his plans mature. In any case, at the end of 1942, he was engrossed in other problems—in two more examples of his cunning.

First, the head of the Sicherheitsdienst was putting the finishing touches to the 'Bernhard' Operation, that is, the production of huge quantities of forged sterling bank-notes. These were to be poured into the coffers of the banks of neutral countries. In this way, real British currency would diminish in value.

Inventive as Schellenberg was in such matters, this plan was not his own. It had been thought up in November 1939 by a certain Alfred Helmuth Naujocks. Schellenberg had been quite fond of Naujocks—it was with him that he had kidnapped Best and Stevens, the two British secret agents, at Venlo, in Holland, on November 8, 1939. It was Naujocks who had 'justified' the invasion of Poland by the Wehrmacht, by carrying out a mock attack on the German radio station at Gleiwitz, on the night of August 31, 1939, with other SS men, disguised like himself as Polish soldiers. His face covered with scars and his nose broken from his fights with German communists before the access to power of the Brown Revolution, A. H. Naujocks was something of an intellectual bully, a subordinate who was somewhat too ambitious and too sly for the taste of Reinhard Heydrich, who had sent him to fight on the Eastern Front in 1942 as a simple SS private.

Schellenberg made various improvements to Naujocks' rather crude plan. The paper needed for the false notes was extremely difficult to imitate: it had to be made from pure linen, soiled, then washed in detergents, without cellulose. It was prepared in the Spechthausen factory at Eberswalde, near Berlin. The engraving of the plates and the printing of the notes was carried out under the direction of Captain Krüger in a secret hide-out: an anonymous shed in the concentration camp at Oranienburg.

The forgery was perfect. Towards the end of 1941, one of Schellenberg's agents changed a large quantity of £5 and £10 notes in Switzerland. He even went so far as to ask for them to be verified, since he said that he had bought them on the black market. The Bank of England kept only 10 per cent of them as suspect and recognised the rest as perfectly genuine. Since then Schellenberg had had the false notes put into circulation in Switzerland, through a certain Dr Willy Gröbl, and particularly in Genoa and Trieste, through an engineer called Friedrich Schwerd. Even when these two cities were no longer under the control of the German Army, the trafficking continued until the end of the war.

The second problem with which Schellenberg was concerned was an espionage affair that was well within his own province—and after the war was to become famous as the

'Cicero' affair. SS-Sturmbannführer Ludwig Moyzisch, who was in charge of the Sicherheitsdienst mission in Ankara, the Turkish capital, had recently sent a message to his chief. He had become very friendly with a certain Eliaza Bazna. Bazna, who was an Albanian, was the valet to the British ambassador, Sir Hughe Knatchbull-Hugessen. This connection promised a rich harvest. Schellenberg replied, urging him to pursue the contact. But how was Bazna, who was proving very greedy, to be paid? Schellenberg hardly hesitated. They would use the wonderful forged currency made at Oranienburg.

With these two dossiers temporarily closed, the SS-Brigadeführer turned once more to Switzerland. Constantly informed by the 'F' bureau in Berne, his main antenna in the Confederation, Schellenberg knew that General Guisan had undertaken a great tour of army messes. The Swiss commander-in-chief took particular pleasure in meeting the ordinary soldiers under his command. In six years, he had travelled 350,000 kilometres throughout his tiny country, either in his Buick, driven by his irreplaceable adjutant Burnens, or in his command-train, consisting of four carriages: a sleeping-car, a restaurant-car, half of which was used as his office, a 2nd-class carriage for the secretaries, and a 3rd-class carriage for the guard.

Schellenberg was also well aware of the anxieties of the head of the Swiss Army. A gloomy-looking Guisan had just spent Christmas of 1942 with the 2nd Regiment of light infantry on the town square of Aarberg, a small township of 2,000 inhabitants half-way between Neuchâtel and Berne. The defence of the redoubts had suffered from disconcerting delays, particularly in the Glaris Alps. Moreover, the lines of pre-defence looked to him to be rather weak, owing to the inadequate number of men mobilised.

In May 1940, Switzerland had 450,000 men mobilised; in August 1940, 145,000; in October 1941, 130,000; in June 1942, after a new attack of the Wehrmacht against the Soviet Union, a mere 70,000; by October 1942, little more than 100,000. This was because the Federal Council regarded mobilisation as a very costly business. In one month the troops consumed as much as in a year in peacetime. If he listened to his strategists, Guisan would none the less demand and maintain general mobilisation until the end of the war. But, of course, there were the civil authorities!

M. Pilet-Golaz, head of the Political Department, was of the opinion that as Switzerland was not threatened by any very precise danger, it would be imprudent at that stage to display Switzerland's total military potential. Such an action could be interpreted as a hostile move against Germany and provoke the Nazis into taking rash action against the Confederation. So Guisan had to be content with speeding up the final defence of his fortresses. The light brigades were to guard the airfields, which would leave the infantry regiments free to reinforce the guards on the trans-Alpine highways. Guisan also decided to bring forward the blackout time in the evening to 8 p.m., instead of 10 p.m. Lastly, he made an urgent request to the Military Department to supply his mountain troops with white camouflage material.

The Swiss people themselves knew nothing of their general's anxieties. The main topic of interest seemed to be the new American film, Wyler's *Mrs Miniver*, with Walter Pidgeon and Greer Garson. It was the first film to deal with the Battle of Britain. The censorship cut only one scene: the conversation between the heroine and a German fighter-pilot in a garden. Schellenberg had promised himself to see the film on his next visit to Switzerland. He was no great lover of the German productions of the UFA. But it was not to see *Mrs Miniver* that he decided, once again, to leave his lair.

On the morning of Saturday, January 30, 1943, an important piece of information reached the Swiss Intelligence headquarters in Lucerne. The preparation and execution of a plan of attack against the Confederation had been entrusted to General Dietl. Dietl, a specialist in winter and mountain operations, who had previously been German commander in Lapland, was training troops near Munich. The same report specified that this army consisted of armoured units, paratroops and *Gebirgsjägers*, or Alpine troops.

General Guisan and Roger Masson reacted in exactly the same way. They did not for a moment doubt the scource of the information. It was the value of the information and its veracity that were so surprising. The latest information concerning the movements of German troops in Austria and Bavaria had arrived the day before. Their agents in Germany had been quite categorical. The number of land forces available were three armoured divisions and six divisions of mountain troops. The air forces were no more than a third of the Luftwaffe, in the whole of western Europe. The rest were engaged on the Russian front. Was this army of Dietl's a piece of bluff, then?

The winter of 1942 was not a happy time for the Third Reich. With half its plumage lost at Tripoli, and badly wounded at Stalingrad, the German eagle no longer soared proudly over the world. It was binding its wounds. In Russia, reverses had forced it to contract its front. And according to General Adolf Heusinger, chief of the 'Operations' section of the OKW, serious psychological errors were beginning to undermine the morale of the Wehrmacht.

"New units are formed," he reported, "while well-tried combat divisions are driven beyond the point of exhaustion. Convalescents and soldiers on leave are taken through units that have not yet seen battle. And they are replaced by reinforcements that are inadequate in both numbers and value. In the most inept way imaginable, the medal for service on the Eastern Front has been given indiscriminately both to men in the rearguard services and to men who have been fighting for a year in snow and ice.

"The whole of the infantry have been renamed 'Grenadiers', when this name should be reserved for only a few units who have given outstanding service. The German Cross, made of gold, looks extremely ugly with its enormous swastika. Lastly, the order whereby the families of men killed on active service are informed by the Party has caused a lot of ill-feeling. The Party has nothing to gain by this."

In short, as Winston Churchill had declared on November 10, 1942, on the BBC: "This is not the beginning of the end, but it is already the end of the beginning."

Moreover, Germany knew, through her spies, that the Swiss 'porcupine' could hold out another two years behind its defences against any army. Masson's organisation had 'overheard' this opinion, expressed by Herr Köcher, the German ambassador in Berne, when it was being radio-telegraphed to Berlin.

The German minister had added that even before the planes carrying the paratroops reached the Swiss frontier, the great tunnels of the Gotthard, Lötschberg and Simplon would be blown up. Switzerland would then no longer provide the invaluable passage through the Alps so coveted by the Wehrmacht. It would become a fortress deprived of strategic importance. Moreover, it would offer no economic advantage: more than a thousand of the country's factories could be blown up at once on orders from Berne. In each of these factories, parts of the machines were painted in different colours according to whether they were to be blown up, smashed or simply detached and taken to a redoubt. Finally, an important point for Germany at a time when the pressure of the Allies was beginning to be felt on the frontiers of Europe, it would not be reasonable to immobilise an army to settle the Swiss 'problem', even if this war was not to last two more years.

"No," Köcher concluded, "such an operation was definitely not to be recommended."

Could it be, then, that the announcement by Dietl of a future invasion of the Confederation was no more than another of Walter Schellenberg's diabolical schemes? A new means of exerting pressure. For a long time, General Guisan and his Secret Service chief, Roger Masson, weighed up their chances. Where was the trap in all this? To ask the Federal Council to declare a general mobilisation after receiving this information would, in any case, be an admission of fear. The only safe and wise solution was to wait. If it was another of Schellenberg's manoeuvres, the SS general would appear on the scene soon enough, when he realised that his plan had not come off. So Guisan simply told Herr Kobelt, the head of the Military Department, of his decision and Roger Masson took due note and did nothing.

It was a judicious decision as it turned out. In the weeks that followed that anxious January 30, 1943, no reports reached Lucerne of the preparation of any army under Dietl. And at the end of February, Schellenberg's assistant, SS-Sturmbannführer Eggen, reappeared. His chief would like to come to Switzerland. Masson had asked for a great deal from him and he had refused him nothing. It was now Schellenberg's turn to make a request: he would like to meet General Guisan. He had only one condition to make about the journey. He would be wearing civilian clothes, of course, but he must absolutely come by plane.

Masson had some difficulty in finding Guisan, who was still touring his troops. On Tuesday March 2 they met in Berne. Would he agree to see the SS general? This must be the great day. Surely, at long last, Schellenberg would reveal what he had in mind. Guisan agreed. Masson decided that the meeting would take place the following day, March 3, at 8 p.m. at the Hôtel Bären, at Biglen.

The Hôtel Bären, a heavy rectangular mass, looked down over the village of Biglen, eighteen kilometres from Berne on the Zürich road that passes through Berthoud and Langenthal. On the front of the hotel, overhanging a square with a chestnut-tree and two fir-trees, there stands a *mutz*, or stone bear, looking very pleased with himself and holding in his front paws three bottles, a large key and a *hannap*.

Brigadier Masson arrived first, driven there by Renaud, his favourite chauffeur. Shortly afterwards, Guisan's Buick arrived, driven by his adjutant Burnens. Schellenberg arrived rather late, accompanied by Captains Meyer and Holzach, who had gone to Berne to meet him. Eggen was also there, as well as two civilians, both security agents of the Sicherheitsdienst.

Very much at ease, the SS general apologised for being late.

"I understand your surprise only too well, gentlemen. You know me to be a friend of the Confederation. I would never of my own accord have taken the liberty of visiting you with an escort. It was entirely at Hitler's insistence. He has become very mistrustful lately! In fact, the Führer had strange misgivings about my coming to Switzerland at all. He was afraid the British Intelligence Service might kidnap me and send me to England, like Rudolf Hess. I told him, of course, that I had nothing to fear in Switzerland. But he insisted that I should be accompanied by these two guardian angels."

Bending towards Guisan and Masson, he went on, in a serious, confidential tone:

"Hitler is also afraid that the Italians know about this visit. If they found out that I had been in Switzerland, they might think it was leading up to an abandonment of the common struggle, at a time when Rommel is making a final, hopeless attempt to defend Tunisia and when, in any case, his recall is seriously being discussed. If the Italians discover my presence here, they might—in the Führer's view—conclude that after the loss of North Africa we were going to abandon the Italian peninsula and make the Alps our line of defence. The Alps would then become the southern boundary of the new Fortress Europa that I would have to force upon you."

Schellenberg paused, head to one side, attentive to the effect his words would produce. Neither Guisan nor Masson said a word. They had simply exchanged a furtive look at the beginning. They were flabbergasted by Schellenberg's latest manoeuvre. The SS general laughed gaily.

"So," he went on, "despite my protestations, and to assuage Hitler's fears, I had to accept this bodyguard and come by plane. But you needn't put up with these men. They can eat in the kitchen."

Guisan protested gently. No, they must all share the same table. The dinner was an exceptionally good one. The landlord of the Hôtel Bären, recognising the commander-in-chief of the Swiss Army, excelled himself. Throughout the meal, Schellenberg was amusing, witty and told stories. Had they heard the latest? Müller, the head of the Gestapo, who disliked Schellenberg intensely, had been spreading a rumour that he exchanged pornographic photographs with Terboven, the Gauleiter of Norway. A rather sinister joke —typical of the spirit now reigning at the head of the régime. Terboven, it is true, is a friend of his, but all the same. . . .

"Each month," he went on, "Hitler meets all his SS generals for dinner. In the course of the last dinner, the Führer raised his glass of mineral water and, pointing his finger at me, laughed. Do you know what he said? He said: 'Let us drink to our young Swissified general.' "

At the end of the meal, Guisan, Masson and Schellenberg retired into one of the lounges. Suddenly, the SS general became serious and attacked. He turned to Masson.

"You have asked me for a certain number of favours. I believe I have always given you what you asked."

He turned suddenly to Guisan. "General, you must now do something for me."

Concealing his anxiety, Masson waited. Erect in his chair, Guisan let his cigar go out.

"I have been sent by the Führer to make a request," Schellenberg went on. "He believes that our recent reverses in Tunisia will be followed by an invasion of Italy. Once again the war will be fought out in Europe. Because of its geographical position, your country could be of great importance for the Allies. The Führer is afraid that Switzerland may not in *all* circumstances, defend its neutrality. He would like to have your assurance that in no circumstances would you allow our enemies' troops to cross your frontiers."

"I find such a suggestion highly offensive!" Guisan interrupted. "Our army will fulfil its mission in *all* circumstances. It will fight whoever violates our territory. Switzerland will remain neutral."

"And yet," Schellenberg objected, "Swiss public opinion is violently anti-German. One only has to read your newspapers."

"A perfectly normal reaction," Guisan replied. "Your own newspapers are constantly attacking us. I repeat no one will be allowed to cross our territory."

"Could you give me a written assurance of this?"

Guisan replied that he could give no such guarantee without the permission of the Federal Council. Nevertheless, he could reassure Schellenberg and Hitler. A week before this meeting he had been interviewed by a Swedish woman journalist who had asked him the same questions. He had given her the same answers. He had a copy of the article in his brief-case. He was willing to sign it. Would that be enough? Unfortunately, he had not his brief-case with him that day. He had left it at his headquarters at Interlaken. The next day he had to go to Arosa, in the Grisons, to supervise a ski-ing competition. If Schellenberg would care to go with him to Arosa, he could give him the 'document' himself.

The SS-Brigadeführer agreed. He was sure that this would be enough to assuage the fears of Field Marshal Keitel and the strategists in the Oberkommando of the Wehrmacht. Guisan, too, seemed satisfied. Only Masson remained apprehensive. Schellenberg could not possibly have created such a build-up for so little. The request he had made, supposedly on Hitler's account, seemed quite derisory. The nearest Allied troops, the Americans and British, were still a thousand kilometres away in North Africa. As for the Russians, they were two thousand five hundred kilometres away.

At this point, Masson realised that Schellenberg was staring at him. Where was the trap, then? For Masson was now sure that there was one. This man was trying to undermine the Swiss leaders' suspicions. To prove this, Masson decided to make yet another request. Since the escape of General Giraud, the Gestapo had arrested the French general's family. Could Schellenberg do something

44

to improve the conditions of these people until they could be freed? In which case Switzerland would be quite ready to give them asylum.

"Certainly!" Schellenberg replied.

Then, after a moment's pause: "Is that really all you have to ask me, brigadier?"

Masson said that it was. Schellenberg looked suddenly disappointed. They sat up late that evening laughing and joking. The SS-Brigadeführer, Eggen and their two guards would now go back to Berne to the rooms they had booked at the Hôtel Bellevue. This was indeed a curious decision on Schellenberg's part—to choose to stay in one of the biggest hotels in Switzerland, when he did not want the Allies or the Italians to know that he was in Switzerland!

It was then that Roger Masson allowed an incident to take place that would enable this 'historic' meeting at Biglen to become known. In other circumstances, the prudence of the brigadier would not have failed him. But Schellenberg's strange behaviour obsessed him. Just as they were about to leave the hotel, the landlord innocently handed round his distinguished visitors' book. Flattered by the presence of General Guisan, he persuaded the general to sign. Masson did the same. And Eggen. Only Captain Meyer realised, shortly afterwards, that these signatures could become compromising in the future. He went back and tore out the page.

The landlord was furious and called in the military police. They, in turn, called in the Federal police. Discreet enquiries were made. In this way Herr Kobelt, head of the Military Department, learnt, on March 24, that the commander-in-chief of the Swiss Army had dined with a leading Nazi, a few kilometres from the Swiss capital, in the middle of a world war. This event did nothing to improve the already cool relations that Guisan had had with the civil authorities of his country since the opening of hostilities.

Masson had been decidedly off-form on that sinister March 3, 1943. But he was to make a second, much more serious mistake. Anxious above all for the safety of his country, he asked Schellenberg, just before the latter set off for Berne, whether it was true that General Dietl was training an army in the Munich region with a view to attacking Switzerland. Did he notice the gleam of triumph in Schellenberg's eye as he asked that question? Schellenberg had wanted proof. Masson had presented him with it on a plate.

The fact that the head of Swiss Intelligence had this piece of information and should want confirmation of it proved that there was a 'leak' in the highest echelons of the Oberkommando of the Wehrmacht, in the very shadow of the Führer himself, and that it found its way to Switzerland, as he had long suspected. The plan of invading Switzerland had been thought up by the SS-Brigadeführer with the sole intention of proving this. Delighted by this ruse, Heinrich Himmler had agreed to go along with Schellenberg's plan. It was he who had insisted that the Wehrmacht should plan such an invasion, without giving any indication that it would never be used. Since Masson knew of the plan, there must be one or several traitors at work in the army head-quarters in Maybach camp, at Zossen, in South Berlin. Schellenberg's next task would be to find out who they were.

Concealing his delight, Schellenberg promised Roger Masson that he would do everything in his power to dis-suade Hitler from attacking Switzerland. However, he would like to see Masson again very shortly.

A quiet meeting was arranged for March 12 in Zürich: the Hôtel Baur au lac, 1, Talstrasse. Schellenberg arrived, after an unbroken thousand-kilometre journey from Berlin, looking tired and anxious. He seemed to suspect enemies everywhere. The Swiss brigadier was able to set his mind at rest by suggesting that they should talk as they paced up and down the promenade. Masson's agents would protect them at a safe distance.

Nobody knows what the two men said to each other on that Friday. All that is known is that Roger Masson's face suddenly changed in expression. His usually mobile features seemed to have frozen. The sharp brightness of his blue eyes, often so warm and lively, seemed to have become dull and expressionless. Those who knew him were aware that this transformation was quite usual with Masson when things were not going the way he wanted them. There was no doubt that Walter Schellenberg had asked him for something that he had had to refuse.

At his trial at Nuremberg in 1949, where he was sentenced to no more than four years' imprisonment, the SS chief was content simply to say of this meeting: "It was my intention to arrange with Masson a kind of regular exchange of information. However, the idea was abandoned, as Masson was unable to agree to it."

He had earlier proved more communicative in London, where, for three years, the British 'treated' him after he had been handed over to them in 1945. During these three years, he had given abundant information concerning his relations with the Swiss to the Intelligence Service agents who had questioned him.

Faithfully describing his series of meetings with Masson, he was to dwell particularly on the one that had taken place in Zürich. He assured Masson that the Führer still persisted in his determination to invade Switzerland. However, he had not yet given up hope of being able to persuade Hitler to give up his plan. But he needed psychological support. The salvation of the Confederation was of incalculable value to him. As someone who, for the past six months, had given innumerable proofs of his friendship, he advised Masson to co-operate with him in his struggle.

Schellenberg then broached the real problem—the problem that had never, in all their previous meetings, been mentioned. The SS general now revealed himself in his true nature—as a past master in the art of blackmail.

This was the problem. As he had often repeated during their visit to Meyer's house at Wolfsberg, he was very concerned about the safety of the Führer. He felt torn between his own feelings and his sense of duty. He knew that within the Oberkommando of the Wehrmacht there were generals who formed a constant nest of intrigue and

47

who would even go so far as to plot against Hitler's life. He was well aware that Masson was using these same men for his own information service. But their days were numbered. The Gestapo, under pressure from Müller, their chief, had built up a convincing body of proof. They would soon be unmasked. He alone, with all the power of his own organisation and his highly placed friends, could still intervene while there was still time. In a few more weeks, it would be too late. By helping these officers, he would be helping Switzerland. But in order to help them, Masson should at once supply him with their names!

Schellenberg was not the kind of man to be disheartened by Masson's refusal. For Walter Schellenberg, failure had no meaning. If one plan failed, he would immediately set about elaborating another. Tirelessly, he continued his assault on Switzerland, willing, as ever, to grant requests. This is proved by the memoirs of Colonel Barbey, Guisan's personal chief of staff. On March 23, 1943, eleven days after the Zürich meeting, B. Barbey notes in his journal:

'Met Masson, who looked particularly pleased. Indeed, more than pleased, actually moved. He has received a message from Eggen, in which Schellenberg says that we have reason "to be pleased with him" . . . The threat of invasion has been lifted. The "Swiss plan" has been *abgeblasen*, abandoned.'

This note proves—if further proof was required—that the brigadier had committed a serious error in letting Schellenberg know of the information that he had received from his agents in Berlin.

In 1945, certain leading Swiss citizens were to reproach Roger Masson for having succumbed to Schellenberg's magnetism. In June 1943, in fact, the Federal Council had to threaten him with severe sanctions to prevent him from going to Berlin to meet Schellenberg. In October 1943, Masson received the German once again for a long weekend at Wolfsberg. Despite numerous protests and an expulsion order drawn up by the Federal Council Masson was to receive Schellenberg's adjutant, Eggen, on Swiss territory, right up to 1945. To suppose from what is known of the facts that Masson was the victim of Schellenberg's stronger personality, is to judge somewhat over-hastily the very delicate situation in which the Swiss officer found himself. It is also to ignore the advantages for the Confederation of having a contact with the Nazis.

Only once did Schellenberg, who on countless occasions had granted Switzerland's requests, himself ask Masson for something. And on that occasion—April 11, 1944—Masson showed how cool, not to say severe, he could be towards the SS general.

Two days before, a German fighter-plane landed at the Swiss military airfield at Dübendorf, near Zürich. The plane was intact. The pilot told the head of the Swiss base that he had landed there on purpose. He had had enough of the war. It was no ordinary fighter-plane, but a Messerschmitt 110, specially equipped for night fighting. It was a prototype that was still secret. Apart from the traditional equipment, it was armed with two vertically-firing 30 mm guns. A formidable machine. On hearing of this catastrophe, Goering flew into a furious rage.

He sent for Schellenberg and ordered him to send at once to Switzerland the head of his commandos of Section VI F, the famous Otto Skorzeny. With thirty men, Skorzeny was to go to Dübendorf and blow up the plane before the Allies discovered it. And this would be easy enough, since ten thousand people a day were coming to admire, from the edge of the airfield, all the American and British bombers which, brought down by the Flak, had had to make forced landings on Swiss territory.

Schellenberg got in touch not with Skorzeny, but with Masson. He knew that an intervention by the excitable Skorzeny at Dübendorf would constitute a veritable *casus belli*. He simply got Masson to have the Messerschmitt 110 destroyed in the presence of the German military attaché in Berne. This was duly done. In exchange for her co-operation, Switzerland was at last allowed to acquire twelve Messerschmitt 109s, which she had coveted for some years.

Twelve Messerschmitt 109s, in April 1944, when the Luftwaffe was being bled on all fronts, two months before the Normandy landing, during which only two German fighters took the air, was a big price to pay for two 30 mm guns, even if they could fire vertically.

To what extent, if at all, did Masson succumb to Schellenberg's magnetism? No one can possibly say. But one fact remains. The chief of Swiss Intelligence never divulged the names of the men who had been working for his organisation—and for others—from the beginning of the war. It was the most extraordinary espionage ring in the whole of the Second World War and bore the fine Nordic name of the 'Viking Line'. A better strategic position than the one it occupied throughout the war could hardly be imagined. It was situated not in some obscure corner of Europe, or even of Germany, but in the very shadow of the Führer himself. It had immediate knowledge of every decision he made. No, Masson could never have presented Walter Schellenberg with such a prize—for one very good reason. Those names—the identities of those German resisters who had refused to bend before Hitler, who were to have such a dramatic effect on the fate of Nazi Germany and who eventually were to drain it of life—those names were entirely unknown to Roger Masson.

differs from all those so far recounted in one important
respect: it is entirely lacking in conventional romanticism.
No women are involved. The few who do move into its
periphery and out again are indistinguishable from the men
they work with. There are no extraordinary raids, carried
out by invincible supermen. It is a story of resistance and
espionage in the raw.

The few strategists who knew of this affair have often
asked themselves since the end of the war: without the
intervention of these men, would Hitler have failed to take
Moscow? Or Stalingrad? Might he not have won the war?
No one, in fact, was better placed than these resisters to have
a decisive influence on the outcome of battles or on the
eventual fate of whole armies. For these men, a mere handful
of German high-ranking officers, attached to army headquarters, belonging to a corps known as the 'amaranth
guild' from the colour of their arm-bands, were members of
the Oberkommando of the Wehrmacht.

What, therefore, was the motive for what, undeniably,

constituted a major act of treason? These patriotic German soldiers abhorred Nazism and hated the Führer.

All the other plots against Hitler, now so well known, failed lamentably—and they failed for one fundamental reason. Their instigators were hesitant men, terrified of their own decisions, ageing soldiers hypnotised by the Nazi phenomenon.

Some of them, as at the time of the bomb-plot of July 20, 1944, General Friedrich Fromm and General Otto Herfurth for example, past masters in the art of not compromising oneself, turned against their fellow-conspirators the day before, hoping in this way to avoid the fury they were helping to unleash. It was Fromm who arrested Hoepner, Olbricht, Stauffenberg, Haeften and Mertz. It was he who drove the ageing General Beck to suicide. He organised a court martial, 'in the name of Hitler', and in the head-lamps of a military car, in the court-yard of the OKW headquarters in the Bendlerstrasse, Berlin, he had the officers he had arrested shot on the spot. But this double betrayal spared neither Herfurth nor Fromm. The first was hanged at Ploetzensee. The second avoided the scaffold, but was shot on March 19, 1945.

In the affair with which we are concerned here, there was no grandiloquence, just a slow, infinitely painstaking determination and effectiveness. These officers of the Oberkommando of the Wehrmacht were fighting not only Hitler but also his mystique, the mystique of the swastika. They knew that their double struggle, which they waged with all the strength at their disposal, would inevitably bring about the defeat of Germany, their Germany. They would continue to work together until Germany lay in ruins around them, until the last vestiges of the Nazi monster had been eradicated. They would then take leave of each other and not meet again. They would no longer have a nation of their own, but at least they would have cleansed it of desecration.

None of these men expected to derive glory from their actions. In their eyes, it was a family affair. Dirty linen that was to be washed in private. This is why it took twenty years before the truth came out. For as soon as their work was done, these Germans retreated at once into anonymity —a judicious precaution. Their incognito preserved them from the ever-active Nazi survivors of the holocaust, among them the mysterious General Reinhard Gehlen, now head of the West German secret service.

The work of these men, which inevitably became the most fascinating resistance and espionage affair of the Second World War, began many years before the war itself. It began, in fact, as early as Easter Sunday, April 17, 1922.

Joseph Stalin, the new General Secretary of the Soviet Communist Party, had recently taken over the leadership of the USSR—it was his task to carry out the plans laid down by Lenin. At Rapallo, an ancient watering-place on the Genoese Gulf on the Italian Riviera, on that same April 17, Germany and the Soviet Republic signed a treaty, re-establishing diplomatic relations between the two countries. Nicolai Krestinski, an ex-lawyer, was to represent the Soviets in Berlin. The distinguished Count Brockdorff-Rantzau was to go to Moscow as the ambassador of the frail Weimar republic, presided over by Friedrich Ebert.

Germany had just lost the Great War. A serious crisis threatened the country. Inflation galloped ahead as the Reichsbank printed bank-notes with an ever-larger format and an ever-increasing number of noughts. The dollar was finally worth 4,200 milliard marks, until Luther, the Finance Minister, and Schacht, the President of the Reichsbank, succeeded in 1924 in stabilising the German currency. Throughout the country, the 'reparations' demanded by the Allies caused bitterness and protests.

The USSR, cut off from the world since the creation of its Communist régime, was hardly better off. It refused to acknowledge the obligations of Imperial Russia or the debts of Tsar Nicolai II. Its economy was suffocating. For the West, after trying in vain to overthrow the régime by military intervention, was now trying to strangle it by a naval blockade.

At Rapallo a defeated and resentful Germany and a USSR with feet of clay recognised each other as equals. They decided to grant each other priority in all commercial transactions. America and Europe may rail at this union of the blind and the paralytic, this 'alliance of poor devils', as Paul Carell called it in his *Operation Barbarossa*, yet Rapallo broke the diplomatic and economic isolation of Europe's down-and-outs. Their transactions were to develop and help them to overcome those dark times. The Soviet Union would buy machines from German firms. Their engineers and business representatives would go backwards and forwards between Moscow and Berlin. German technicians would get good jobs in Soviet mines and electrical installations. Gradually, the Allies would have to realise that this pact was not as mad as they had thought. But they would have shuddered indeed had they discovered what was going on between Germany and Russia.

Since Rapallo enabled the two countries to break the quarantine imposed on them by other nations, why not apply the spirit and the letter of the treaty to more serious matters?—the military blockade as far as the USSR was concerned and the prohibitions of the Treaty of Versailles in the case of Germany. The Red Army lacked cadres and method. No military school would agree to providing it with the necessary training. Germany had neither tanks nor heavy guns, neither an air force nor a navy. Its tiny army, limited to 100,000 men, was unable to train properly. In Moscow, Radek was thinking up a coalition that was to surreptitiously blow open the locked doors of the West:

"Place the experience of German officers at the disposal of the new Soviet army; and help to rebuild the completely destroyed Russian war machine. In exchange, the Soviet Union will manufacture the arms that the Reichswehr is forbidden to possess. The Reichswehr will also train with these arms on Russian soil."

Karl Radek was a journalist on *Izvestia*. He was an expatriate, born in Poland. He had a brilliant mind and was regarded by Leon Trotsky as his best colleague. Radek had just been appointed director of Soviet propaganda and was already calling for "the struggle of the Comintern against the Treaty of Versailles and against the capitalist offensive."

In Moscow, supporters of Stalin were spreading the rumour that Radek's brilliant initiative had been suggested to him by Colonel Nicolai, head of the Reichswehr intelligence service and a great friend of Trotsky's. Both Trotsky and Radek were strongly suspected of deviationism. But such political differences were not, at the moment, of the greatest importance. What mattered was that the Red Army should obtain as soon as possible the cadres it so sadly lacked. So in Berlin the Soviet ambassador, Nicolai Krestinski, made discreet approaches to General von Seeckt, the head of the Reichswehr, and to Gessler, the German Defence Minister. A flow of secret agreements resulted.

Each year, until 1930, a third of the annual budget of the Reichswehr, plus one hundred and twenty million 'stabilised' marks, went into a strange cartel: the *Gesellschaft zur Förderung gewerblichen Unternehmen*, the Industrial Enterprises Development Corporation. This company had two offices: one in Berlin and a second, more important one, in Moscow. It dealt directly with the Soviet government and had a number of sub-contracting branches throughout the Soviet Union. Junker planes were produced at Fili and Samara, on the border of Central Siberia; shells at Tula and Slatust; poison gas at Krasnogvardeisk; submarines and even a battleship in the shipyards of Leningrad.

Moreover, three large practice bases were prepared for the use of the German Army. Two of these, at Lipezk and Voronej, were intended for the air force. The third, at Kazan, on the middle reaches of the Volga, was for the tank corps. It was there that the 'black' Reichswehr carried out its exercises—20,000 strong in all, chosen from among the best combatants of the Great War, the future officers and non-commissioned officers of the Wehrmacht. Before leaving for Russia, each of these soldiers was to have his name 'erased' from the army lists. On his return, he would quite simply be reinstated—a cunning camouflage.

It was a fantastic undertaking. Prototypes of planes and tanks, developed in Germany's secret workshops, went in parts to the USSR, via the free port of Stettin. They were unloaded in Leningrad. They were then assembled and tested; finally, they were mass-produced in Soviet factories. The first Jabos fighter-bombers, the first types of Stukas, and the future Focke-Wulf were all developed on the banks of the Don and used in Red Army exercises.

It was also from Stettin that the troops of the 'black' Reichswehr set off for Russia. And to Stettin were brought the remains of those German soldiers who had been killed in the rigorous training exercises they had undergone. They were transported in hermetically sealed zinc containers. This remarkable organisation was the work of General Kurt von Schleicher. Without Lipezk, Hermann would never have been able to muster all the élite pilots that were to transform the Luftwaffe into such a formidable force. Without Kazan, the armoured divisions of Guderian, Hoepner and Hoth would never have acquired the attack that was to make them the spearhead of the Wehrmacht.

On the other hand, the young Soviet soldiers selected to become commanding officers and the political commissars, chosen for the same reasons, trained side by side with the cadets of the Reichswehr. Side by side they learnt the art of war from men like Moltke, Clausewitz and Ludendorff. The governments of the two countries pursued different political aims, but in the field their soldiers were on very good terms.

General Hans von Seeckt, embittered by the Treaty of Versailles, which he did not hesitate to call a calamity, cherished a plan of revenge: to strike Poland. With this country, an outpost of France in eastern Europe, one of the important pillars of that detested peace would collapse. But to achieve this, he needed the help of the Russians.

This plan, and the strongly anti-Western spirit that motivated it, delighted the head of the Red Army, Marshal Mikael Tukhachevsky, and its potential high command, Generals Yakir, Kork, Uborevich and Feldman—who were later to fall with him in Stalin's purges. Tukhachevsky believed von Seeckt and was unreservedly in favour of his plan—because Poland was an embarrassment to Russia too, and also because his high command, who professed an almost servile admiration for German militarism, considered that an alliance between Germany and the Western powers was to be prevented at all costs. A new armed intervention of this kind would place Russia in mortal danger.

It is easy to understand why no Russian or German military leader could envisage the possibility, let alone the plan, of a Germano-Soviet war before Hitler came to power. Such a conflict would have been regarded as fratricide between two high commands that had grown up together.

One man was to make an objective inquiry into pro-Russian feeling in the German Army among the Junker caste and the officer corps, after the First World War— Walter Schellenberg. In 1937, Heydrich, head of the Sicherheitsdienst, whom he was to replace five years later, gave him the job of making a study of the past relations between the Reichswehr and the Red Army.

"These relations were marked," Schellenberg wrote, "by what I shall call the *spirit of Tauroggen*. I am referring to the alliance directed against Napoleon in 1812, signed in the village of Tauroggen in East Prussia, between the Prussian general, Yorck von Wartenburg, and the Russian Army, despite the express orders of the king of Prussia. It is interesting to note that the Prussian military organisation against Napoleon had been prepared in Russia, where they had found refuge under the protection of the Tsar, by Baron von Stein and Clausewitz. . . . The pursuit of the policy of co-operation with Russia was of vital importance for the implementation of Bismarck's foreign policy. The treaty of Rapallo marked a return to this policy."

The spirit of Tauroggen—this was the spirit that motivated that group of officers who, in the midst of the Ober-kommando of the Wehrmacht, were to work for the destruction of Hitler and Nazism. There were eleven of them in all. They were Bavarians and Protestants: all from families in which, traditionally, only two careers could be contemplated, the civil service and the army.

Their names are known to very few people. To make them public would, even today, bring the opprobrium of the new Germany upon their families, even, perhaps, expose them to reprisals of an unforeseeable seriousness. There must be many people in West Germany who believe that these men, who hampered the operations of the Wehrmacht —out of hatred for Nazism—by betraying the secrets of these operations, thus sabotaging its military capacity, stabbed the German combatants in the back, and caused incalculable losses of both men and materials. This is why we shall give only the initials of these enemies of the 'Brown' revolution, confirming only the identity of their leader—because he devoted his whole life to the struggle against the Nazi mystique.

Nothing predisposed Rudolf Roessler to conspiracy—or to treason, as some would have it—any more than it did his ten companions: Helmuth S, Hermann F, Rudolf G, Fritz T and Georg T, who were to become generals. O became a colonel and K a major. The last three, S, A and O, reached the rank of captain.

Although he had not chosen, like the other ten, to become a career officer, Rudolf Roessler none the less came from the same background, the same social class. His family was one of those conventional, middle-class German families, hostile to any spirit of adventure, in which one soon learns that order means bread and disorder famine.

The Roesslers came from Kaufbeuren, a former imperial free-city, medieval in atmosphere, but now one of Bavaria's industrial centres, situated on the Wertach and possessing a population of 23,000. The father, a local dignitary and a senior civil servant in the Ministry of Waters and Forests, brought his children up in the Protestant faith. Rudolf's elder brother took up law and became a public prosecutor; his sister became a teacher at the Gymnasium in Augsburg, also in Bavaria.

Rudolf Roessler first met his ten companions at the Front in the First World War and they became firm friends. The other ten were from one of those military academies where young cadets are turned into loyal and efficient officers, and where individualists are soon crushed into the required shape—where, too, a good grounding in literature and philosophy is inculcated. They readily adopted the 'civilian' Roessler, who had volunteered at the age of seventeen. They liked his extensive knowledge and his artistic tastes. He was to become their intellectual leader and their contact with real life. He was to show them wider horizons than those of the barrack walls.

Then came defeat—a time of doubt and despair. The German Army was broken up and humiliated, and fell into the hands of soldiers' committees. Institutions seemed to be collapsing all around them. The Weimar Republic tottered between the thrusts of the extreme right and the extreme left. *Coups d'état* followed one after another, violent and short-lived. In Berlin the Red Week caused one thousand two hundred deaths between March 4 and 13, 1919. In Munich, the headquarters of the Communist Party went up in flames. The fall of the mark ruined the middle classes, while gigantic trusts, like that of Hugo Stinnes, were being built up.

A new Right-wing movement, much more extreme than any that had appeared so far, was born in Bavaria: National Socialism. There were some dubious characters at its head—Dietrich Eckart, a journalist; an ex-sergeant major, Max Amann; two other soldiers, Rudolf Hess, an ex-lieutenant, and Ernst Roehm, an ex-captain, flanked an ex-corporal, a street-corner orator called Adolf Hitler. Most of his support came from the working class. His fanaticism alarmed the middle classes. Five years of fear and chaos followed until the death in 1925 of the President, Friedrich Ebert, and his succession by the reassuring figure of Marshal Hindenburg, the very symbol of tradition. The various Right-wing groups united behind him. Meanwhile, Hitler was building up his forces.

Rudolf Roessler was a small, thin, quiet man, but his eyes were bright, intelligent and very mobile. He wore thin-rimmed glasses. He had now left the army—violence horrified him. While retaining his Right-wing opinions, he had become a pacifist. But he no longer hoped that society could be reformed without revolutionary methods. The rise of Nazism, which he had carefully observed and analysed, terrified him. Germany was asleep, enveloped in a false sense of security—after all, had not the Allies evacuated the Ruhr? And was not prosperity returning with leaps and bounds? Roessler decided that at all costs he must try and awaken his fellow-countrymen to the danger within. He joined the *Augsburg Post Zeitung* as a journalist and became the scourge of Nazism. He met his army friends more than ever before and took part with them in the great processions organised by the *Stahlhelm*, the 'Steel Helmet'. He tried to convey to them his fear of the 'Brown' revolution. But they gently ridiculed his apprehensions.

They were members of the Reichswehr. When, in 1920, General Hans von Seeckt tried to save the Weimar Republic by depriving the army of all political influence, they signed on for twelve years, which allowed them to be among the 'Hundred Thousand'. Did not the Reichswehr—that haven of peace and discipline—harbour enough enemies of disorder. The Nazis could do nothing, they argued. They had been crushed in 1923.

Had Roessler forgotten? they asked. While he had been fighting the Brownshirts with his pen, they had fought them in the street. They had been among the troops who had encircled Roehm, the SA chief, in the War Ministry, in the Schoenfeldstrasse in Munich, at the time of Hitler's abortive putsch in November. And what was the result? The Nazi Party was dissolved, then made legal again, and now it was dying out. At the last election, it didn't even get a million votes; twelve seats in the Reichstag out of 491.

Roessler should not worry. Hitler's crazy ideas would not catch on, they reassured him. They confided also that although General von Seeckt had forbidden his soldiers to participate in elections they had other much more effective ways of working for the revival of Germany's great past. One after another, they were to leave for Russia, for Lipezk and Kazan, where they would train with weapons that the Reichswehr were 'forbidden' to possess.

This prospect of a national revival did not assuage Rudolf Roessler's fears. While continuing to frequent his small circle of army friends, he took refuge in the study of theology and other subjects. He became a friend of Nicolai Berdiaiev, the Russian philosopher of freedom, a critic of rationalism, who was very concerned for the spiritual condition of modern man. He also met Karl Barth, the Swiss theologian, then professor at the University of Münster, Westphalia.

Finally, Roessler became secretary of the *Bühnenvolksbund*, an organisation devoted to the spread of the theatre, and director of the magazine *Das National Theater*, in Berlin. Meanwhile, his small circle of military friends had all obtained good positions at the Reichswehr headquarters. And it was through them that Roessler's intellectual influence reached its peak, when he was invited to join the very select *Herrenklub*, in the Vosstrasse in Berlin. Up to the crisis that overtook the Reichswehr in 1930, Rudolf Roessler was to give no less than two thousand lectures there.

With the Wall Street crash, the Weimar Republic was once again on the verge of ruin. Its economy, which was based on American loans and on exports, collapsed. Unemployment mounted. The army received its first great setback.

On September 20, 1930, the ten friends of 'RR'—as they called Roessler among themselves—woke with a start. Deaf to his innumerable warnings, they had not noticed the brown ants nibbling away at their bastion. Suddenly, on that day, the ground collapsed from under them. There was to be an important trial before the Leipzig Supreme Court: three lieutenants from the garrison at Ulm, Scheringer, Wendt and Ludin, were accused of spreading Nazi propaganda within the Reichswehr. Membership of Hitler's party was enough to exclude any prospective soldier from membership of the 'Hundred Thousand'. This had been decided by old General von Seeckt. The edict also included civilians working in the arsenals and military stores. There were to be no Fascists in the army. Yet, despite this, the officer corps, particularly its younger elements, had been shown to have become contaminated. But Scheringer, Wendt and Lubin were also accused of a much more serious crime: high treason. They had tried to persuade their fellow soldiers not to open fire on Hitler's supporters in the event of an armed uprising on their behalf.

General Groener, the Defence Minister, wanted to have the lieutenants brought before a simple court martial, in order to avoid unsavoury publicity. But Scheringer had secretly alerted the *Völkischer Beobachter*, the Nazi news-paper. Everything would take place in the open, and the trial would reveal how far the gangrene had reached.

Adolf Hitler, cited as a witness for the defence, could hardly hope for a better public platform. For a long time he had been waiting for an opportunity to dissipate the mistrust instinctively felt by the Reichswehr towards him. He would captivate the army with his favourite tactic, of which he was a past master: the lie. The fate of the three young lieutenants was of little concern to him compared with his wider aim—gaining the support of the officer corps. He would simply disown his three disciples, in order to reassure the others.

"These three young men were quite wrong," he declared, "to believe that we would ever contemplate armed rebellion. We will use only constitutional means to gain power. I will never fight the army. Quite the contrary. When the government of our country is in my hands—which will be in a matter of months—I shall regard you, gentlemen, as the essential nucleus from which the great army of the German people will emerge."

Lost among the crowd of spectators, all of them soldiers, the friends of Rudolf Roessler were struck with terror at the hypnotic power of this street politician's arguments: their colleagues appeared to be lapping up his reassuring words.

In that troubled time most of the soldiers of the

Reichswehr were lacking in confidence, in a sense of purpose. Many of them were beginning to wonder whether this National-Socialism, which was regarded as a danger, and which claimed to be capable of assuming the destiny of the nation, might not after all be what the German people needed to restore the former greatness of Germany—and to shake off the humiliating shackles imposed on them by the Treaty of Versailles. As if he guessed the hopes of his audience, Hitler went on:

"Germany is bound hand and foot by the peace treaties. We National-Socialists do not regard these treaties as having the force of law. They were forced upon us. We cannot accept that our sons, who are innocent, should remain under this yoke. If we protest against these treaties with every means at our disposal, we will find ourselves on the road to revolution."

Hitler declaimed his speech with one hand on his heart, the other brandished with clenched fist. It had its effect. A cold shudder passed through the court-room, followed by tumultuous applause. The minutes of the trial leave no doubt of this. Looking back, it seems inconceivable that the Leipzig judges could have tolerated such a manifestation. But the event must be seen in its historical context. Perhaps they too were impressed by Hitler's speech. Most of the audience on that occasion were impressed and felt suddenly well disposed towards a political movement that declared itself ready, according to its leader, to support the army, instead of sapping its strength as they had feared. Hitler restrained his delight. He had taken in the Reichswehr completely. They would pay for it later, *en masse*.

The sentences passed on the three condemned lieutenants, eighteen months each, satisfied nobody. For those who sympathised with Hitler it was too heavy; for the others, far too light. If the judges had acted with greater severity and respected the rules and discipline of the Reichswehr, they would have done much to revive the confidence of the army. It would no doubt have recovered quickly enough from the shock it had experienced while listening to Hitler.

The hesitancy of the Leipzig judges completely demoralised the army. It was hopelessly divided by the activities of the ever more numerous and ever more arrogant supporters of Hitler. Even General Hans von Seeckt himself, though later deprived of his functions, was for a time a supporter of Hitler and insisted that his sister should vote for the ex-corporal rather than for Marshal Hindenburg.

On the evening of September 20, 1930, Roessler and his small circle weighed up the situation. They now felt certain that, exasperated by the weaknesses of the Weimar republic and with nothing in their bellies, the whole of the German people were willing to embark on an era of madness. They would make the worst possible choice, Nazism, the negation of German culture. They would give their support to men who spouted a confused mass of unassimilated notions and who would act as merciless butchers. Hitler had said as much during the Leipzig trial. It had slipped out during his interrogation by the president of the tribunal:

"I can assure you that when the National-Socialist movement is victorious, there will be a national-socialist court of justice. Our revolution will take its revenge and heads will fall!"

No reasonable man could lend his support to these future masters of Germany, thought Roessler's friends. On the contrary, he should fight against it quite ruthlessly.

There was little time left for them to prepare their secret resistance, to work out their plans in detail. Events were rushing ahead. Thirty-four months after the Leipzig trial, on July 14, 1933, the Nazi Party, now completely in power in Germany, decreed a law.

"The National-Socialist Party of German Workers is the only legal political party in Germany. Whoever tries to preserve or found any other political party will be condemned to a maximum sentence of three years' hard labour or from six months to three years in prison, unless the crime is punishable by more serious penalties under the terms of other laws."

Hitler had triumphed. He had destroyed all legal

opposition. A month later, in August 1933, Rudolf Roessler met a young Swiss citizen in Berlin: Xavier Schnieper. Schnieper was twenty-three years old, the son of an important magistrate in the canton of Lucerne. Because of his Left-wing ideas he was regarded as the black sheep of the family. He was studying for his doctorate in philosophy and was passionately concerned for the upheavals that he foresaw in Europe. Anyone with his eyes open could see what would happen by looking at how the Nazis had come to power. And there was no better vantage-point than Berlin. It was there that he became friendly with the director of the revue *Das National Theater*, which was rather too Right-wing for his tastes. But he liked Rudolf Roessler himself. He had a mind of his own, this man who was for ever repeating Luther's words, "I am standing and cannot do otherwise."

Very soon, however, Schnieper realised from his conversation with Roessler, that this little man was capable of far more than writing articles for a theatre revue. What, he did not yet know. But it was he who suggested to Roessler that he should go and settle in Switzerland, where he would be safe. Roessler did not hesitate. With his wife, Olga, and only ten marks in his pocket—it was the most that could be taken out of Germany at that time—he caught the train for Lucerne. What did money matter? Peace of mind would make the bread of exile less bitter.

When all the officers of the army high command were compelled shortly afterwards to take the oath of allegiance to the Führer, before General von Fritsch, in the great hall of the Reichswehr Ministry, on the Tirpitz embankment, in Berlin, Roessler's ten friends did not give themselves away. But at the same time among themselves, they each made another promise: to do everything in their power to defeat Hitler and Nazism.

Germany was entering its dark night of madness. Yet a delicate thread linked them to the free world, to light. At the end of this thread was their friend Rudolf. A thousand kilometres away, he was waiting, ready to be of use.

5

FROM 1934, RUDOLF ROESSLER
lived with his wife, Olga, in Wesemlin, a suburb of Lucerne,
four kilometres from the city centre, where they rented a
small flat. Every morning, punctually at 7.30, he arrived at
a small publishing house situated among the winding streets
of the old town—the Vita Nova Verlag, of which Roessler
was the manager until his death in 1958. It had been founded
by a group of his Swiss friends. The Vita Nova Verlag, at
36 Fluhmattstrasse, no longer exists, but Roessler's colleagues are still living in Lucerne.

Day after day, with obstinate patience, Rudolf Roessler
devoted himself to his task. In article after article and
pamphlet after pamphlet, he exposed with extreme virulence
the ravages that Hitler's religion was inflicting on Germany.
The 'ammunition' for his writings came, of course, from
Berlin. Almost every day he received a letter from one of his
German friends, in which confidential information was
concealed in innocent-seeming language. Sometimes, too,
one of the ten would come and visit Roessler in Lucerne.

Thanks to them, Roessler announced a month in advance

the occupation by the Wehrmacht on March 7, 1936, of the demilitarised zone of the Rhineland. He exposed the events leading up to the fall of General Werner von Fritsch and the seizure of Austria. But above all he published political analyses in which he lay bare the true nature of the new, aggressive, prosperous Germany that so impressed the Western democracies.

Roessler and his ten friends could not accept as their own this new Germany that arrested thousands of Catholic priests and Protestant pastors, that disbanded the Christian youth movements and forbade the publication of any works of a spiritual nature, that burnt tens of thousands of books that 'poisoned the roots of German thought', that controlled every sphere of the country's cultural life, that excluded the Jews from artistic activity and destroyed six thousand five hundred works of art which the Nazis regarded as decadent.

They attacked the Nazification of education, the falsification of history and the degeneration of the sciences. They hated this Germany that banned non-Nazi newspapers, turned journalists into officials of the Propaganda Ministry and exercised strict control over the cinema; that returned to a feudal-type system of agriculture in which the peasant was confined to his piece of land and his work rigorously controlled; that reduced the industrial worker to the level of a serf, controlled the movement of labour and increased income tax; that had Nazified its entire civil service and legal profession; that had set up the dreadful People's Courts and had opened fifty concentration-camps since 1934.

Swiss readers might well be astonished by the revelations of this inexhaustible anti-Fascist who signed himself R. A. Hermes. What was the real identity of the man behind the pseudonym? Why Hermes? Hermes was the son of Zeus, but, much more to the point, he was the Messenger of the Gods! The choice of name was no accident. And from about the middle of 1939 Roessler's role as messenger was suddenly to take on quite different proportions—so much so that his previous literary work was to seem of comparatively small moment. On May 23, in Berlin, an event took place that was to have profound historical significance.

That day the Führer called a meeting of his army chiefs at the Chancellery. Hitler seemed nervous. The day before he had signed the Steel Pact whereby the fate of Italy was inextricably linked with that of Germany. Opposite him sat fourteen officers, including Goering and General Milch for the Luftwaffe, Admiral Raeder and Rear-Admiral Schniewind for the Kriegsmarine and Keitel, Brauchitsch and Halder for the Wehrmacht.

Hitler wasted no time in discussion. As William L. Shirer remarks in *The Third Reich*, none of those officers left the Chancellery that day without a very clear idea of what was going to happen by the end of the summer.

"No more victories can be won without bloodshed," Hitler declared, according to the notes of the meeting made by Lieutenant-Colonel Schmundt. "We must expand to the East in order to guarantee our food supplies and also to resolve the problem of the Baltic States. There is no other course to be taken in Europe. If we are forced by fate to come to grips with the West, the possession of a vast territory in the East will be an incalculable advantage. There can be no question of sparing Poland. We shall attack her at the first favourable opportunity. War will break out.

"If Great Britain and France support Poland, then they too must be attacked. Dutch and Belgian air-bases must be occupied militarily. Declarations of neutrality cannot be respected. We must make a lightning attack on Holland. Our aim must be the establishment on Dutch territory of a defence-line going right up to the Zuyderzee. The war with Britain and France will be a fight to the death. The idea that we shall be able to avoid this is a dangerous one. It will no longer be a matter of being right or wrong, but whether or not there are to be eighty million Germans."

The fourteen officers sat in silence, hypnotised. Not one dared to interrupt Hitler's exposition. Already, in 1937, the Führer had suggested similar plans of aggression to his military chiefs. Von Blomberg and von Fritsch protested, on the grounds that Germany lacked the forces necessary to win a European war. But von Blomberg and von Fritsch were no longer there. This time Hitler was not making suggestions, he was giving orders. He digressed on the subject of Britain and the character of the British people. This is what haunted him—the British lion. He repeated himself, as if he was trying to convince himself of the rightness of his decision. Finally, the Führer ordered his officers to pay particular attention to the outlines he would give them of a strategic plan that they were to work out in more detail:

"The objective must be to strike the enemy a crushing and absolutely decisive blow from the beginning. No consideration of right or wrong, or of treaties, must interfere with the execution of the plan. We must make preparations both for a long war and for a surprise attack. Any possible intervention by Britain on the Continent must be stopped at once. The army must occupy the positions essential to the navy and to the Luftwaffe. If we succeed in occupying Holland and Belgium, together with France, we shall have the bases for a victorious war against Britain. Taking off from the west of France the Luftwaffe will be able to exert a strict blockade against Britain. And the blockade will be completed by our submarines.

"The decisive condition for success is secrecy. I shall reveal my objectives neither to Italy nor to Japan. And I regret to say that I cannot entirely trust my High Command. Our plans must not be communicated to them. Form a small commission within the OKW, whose task it will be to draw up the military details of the plan."

Perhaps Hitler was already suspicious. German agents in Switzerland sifted every word that was published concerning German problems. Naturally, they had read the writings of the mysterious Hermes. Yet the information published by him did not constitute a betrayal of defence secrets. This declaration by the Führer of May 23 could be due to nothing more than his instinctive mistrust. However, his fears were fully justified.

On May 30, two Germans in civilian dress got out of the train at Lucerne. They had come from the Reich. They were Generals Fritz T and Rudolf G, the 'leaders' of the small conspiracy in Berlin. Rudolf Roessler took the precaution of receiving them, not in the bookshop, but at his home at Wesemlin—the Vita Nova Verlag might be watched by German spies.

"It's all over!" Rudolf G began. "War will break out in a matter of weeks, three months at the latest. Hitler decided on it on the 23rd of this month."

"Are you sure?" Roessler asked after a brief silence.

"Positive! The Führer has never entirely trusted the Oberkommando of the Wehrmacht. He wants the job of drawing up the Wehrmacht's plans of attack to be limited to a small commission. Brauchitsch and Halder have just asked us to join it." He continued, emphatically: "Nazi Germany must not win this war."

"Has she any chance of winning it?" Roessler asked.

"Who knows? Thomas, the economic chief of the OKW, has just produced his estimates. In four years, the Wehrmacht has expanded from seven to fifty-one divisions. The Luftwaffe has twenty-one squadrons and 270,000 highly trained men. Not enough, of course, to take on the whole of Europe. But Hitler's going to try and break up the conflict into manageable pieces. He'll begin with Poland. This will give him time to continue the military build-up before attacking the West. German industry is expanding at a colossal rate. And it is working entirely for the army. If it is not beaten at once the Wehrmacht will become a lethally powerful instrument. Hitler is taking a chance. He is convinced that Britain and France will not stand in his way."

"The break has come," murmured Roessler, after another short silence.

"We shall win," Rudolf G went on excitedly. "We shall bleed this Germany that we have disowned to its death, so that our Germany may be reborn. You know why we joined the Wehrmacht when it superseded the Reichswehr: we were waiting for an opportunity. Brauchitsch and Halder have given it to us. We are already in posts of vital importance—in Operations, Logistics, Transport, Military Economy and Communications. All we needed was this latest post. Try as they may, the Nazis cannot do without experts. They have to admit that at least the Reichswehr knew how to train soldiers. Well, all this will be very useful. But not quite in the way the Nazis expect. We shall send you all the information of any importance. Use it as you think fit. Give it away or sell it, as you wish—and to whom you wish. But preferably to the staunchest enemies of Nazism."

Rudolf Roessler regarded the two generals in silence. At last, he said: "You realise where this will lead you. Once we have begun, there'll be no turning back. You realise this?"

It was Rudolf G who replied: "Of course. Don't forget that you have always acted as our conscience. We now need you more than ever before. We shall not be able to see or even write to each other for long. So Fritz will explain to you how we shall communicate with each other from now on."

General Fritz T had been able to get a small trunk through the customs at Basle. It was a great risk, of course, but it was the only way—time was running out. The trunk contained radio-telegraphic equipment: a short-wave transmitter-receiver, one of the latest models issued only to the Wehrmacht. Fritz T had taken it in the form of spare parts from the stores of the broadcasting department. It had been an easy matter to get hold of the instructions for assembling the set and to falsify the stock figures. Did Roessler have a friend in Switzerland that he could trust, who would be capable of putting the equipment together and who knew enough morse to be able to act as operator?

Roessler did know someone who fitted this description—a German émigré called Christian Schneider, who was working for the International Labour Office in Geneva. But Roessler would simply ask Schneider to assemble the set and teach him how to operate it. He would do the transmitting himself. The fewer people involved in a conspiracy, the better.

Fritz T agreed. He handed the equipment over to Roessler, with the codes and lists of wave-lengths that would be used. Roessler's friends had meticulously laid their plans. Eight of them, simply by virtue of their posts, were at the very source of information concerning the Wehrmacht's movements. Each transmission of news concerning the army would be preceded by the word *Werther* —simply because the first two letters of Goethe's work are also those of the Wehrmacht. The other two conspirators, high-ranking officers in the Luftwaffe, would communicate any information concerning the air force, but it would pass through the same channel as the other. This news would be announced by a different signal, *Olga*—this being the name of Roessler's wife.

How had it come about that the Oberkommando of the Wehrmacht allowed such an important and continuous 'leak' to be set up so easily and to remain undetected? A great many observers have remarked that as the war continued, the OKW became more like a public meeting than a powerful and disciplined ant-hill. By taking over on February 4, 1938, the posts of supreme commander of the Wehrmacht, War Minister and commander-in-chief of the Wehrmacht, Hitler wanted to concentrate all his forces in his own hands. As a result, he engendered a monster that never grew up.

In 1925, under the iron rule of General Hans von Seeckt, the Reichswehr command comprised no more than 220 high-ranking officers—assisted, it is true, by a large batallion of civil servants. By 1933, this number had doubled. In 1939, the Wehrmacht High Command seemed as if it was struck by an absolutely irresistible tendency to expansion. There were now 2,000 officers of all ranks and 7,000 civil servants. This swelling of numbers at the OKW was to continue at a rapidly increasing rate until, in 1940, there were double the number of army officers wearing the purple stripe down their trousers.

This was because each of the commanding officers appointed by the Führer brought his own contingent of assistants with him, which he duly added to those of his predecessor—and which, in turn, he left to his successor when he moved on. There were, therefore, strata of every loyalty and shade of opinion. A superficial examination of the OKW quickly reveals who were von Seeckt's men, von Blomberg's or von Fritsch's—or Beck's, von Brauchitsch's, Halder's, Zeitzler's, Guderian's and Krebs'. In addition, there were the favourites of the moment, appointed as a simple demonstration of faith in Nazism by Keitel, Jodl or Hitler himself. This mass of officers were crushed into the offices on the Tirpitz embankment, the Wilhelmstrasse, the Bendlerstrasse and in Maybach camp at Zossen at the gates of Berlin. The cleverest of these officers succeeded in getting themselves appointed to the Führer's own headquarters, which followed Hitler wherever he went.

The OKW swarmed with mutually antagonistic clans, and festered with repressed jealousy and rancour. The great thing was to avoid any serious responsibility and therefore any chance of making an irremediable mistake, which would be enough to get one sent to active service on the front. The whole organisation was under constant supervision by Gestapo agents.

Outside this world of intrigue and violent internal convulsions were a number of technicians, more interested in their work of improving the efficiency of the Wehrmacht than in attending parades and receptions. Among these were Roessler's ten friends. The surrounding anarchy, produced by an over-concentration of power, acted as a perfect screen for their activities. It was easy enough for them to obtain the strategic plans and the details of the Wehrmacht's movements because they were among the men who produced them. They were then transmitted to Rudolf Roessler from the official broadcasting centre of the OKW!

Inside this building were two huge halls that buzzed permanently, night and day, with noise from about a hundred transmitter-receivers. On one side were a long row of small offices housing the coding technicians. It was they who held the keys to the OKW dispatches. The wireless operators knew nothing. They simply transmitted, uncomprehendingly, the long series of cabalistic letters they were given, taking note of the times and wavelengths indicated in the margin of every message. In the same way, they wrote down, without the slightest idea of their meaning, the floods of mysterious dots and dashes they received.

Fritz T was one of the assistants of General Fellgiebel, the head of the whole Communications department. He had practically the whole of the centre under his own control. There were a number of wireless operators he could depend on—among them two sergeants, who had good reason to be grateful to him. Nothing ever surprised them and they never asked questions. In turn, they transmitted the messages of *Werther* and *Olga*, without knowing in the least what or to whom they were communicating—T having coded everything beforehand, and Roessler being but one correspondent among many others, known as RAHS, his call number.

Fritz T did everything possible to reduce the chances of discovery. He insisted that his transmission should never, except in exceptional circumstances, last longer than half an hour. The longer dispatches were to be broken up and spread over several days if necessary. Rudolf Roessler was never to call either of the two sergeants. This would be done only when they were on leave and just before they returned. The messages would then be handed to T as soon as the sergeants were back at their posts.

In the event of an unexpected silence on Roessler's part—which would mean that something had happened to him—*Werther* and *Olga* would refrain from making any attempt to contact him. It would be up to Roessler to re-establish contact. He would do this by sending out his signal 'RAHS' several days in succession at midnight. It would then be for his friends in Berlin to contact him. The plan had its risks of course, but it was one that had a very good chance of success. However, if the break came from Berlin, Roessler could do nothing more than pray for the safety of his friends. A prolonged silence would mean that the Gestapo had got hold of everybody!

The machine could now be turned on. They had only to await the Führer's decisions to feed into it. Each of these decisions would be turned against him and contribute to his ultimate, irrevocable fall. He would thus destroy himself. This simple, meticulous plan could not fail. Its results would not, of course, be evident at once. There would be no sudden, spectacular reversals. But in time they would do their work.

Only one outstanding point remained to be settled—and it was no detail. How and to whom was the mass of information that would soon begin to flow be given? It was up to Rudolf Roessler to resolve this problem. For a long time, he considered his options. Go round the Allied embassies with his wares under his arm? No one would take him seriously. He would be dismissed as an *agent-provocateur*. There was only one solution—Switzerland. She had generously taken him in in 1933. If she thought fit, she would distribute the information among the relevant nations. Roessler dared not admit to himself that he would be offering his hostess a poisoned present. For if she did as he wished, she would be jeopardising her neutrality.

A few days after his two compatriots had returned to Berlin, Roessler arranged to meet Xavier Schnieper. The young Swiss had also become one of his close friends. However, Roessler was careful not to entrust him with the whole truth of what he was doing: the most devoted friend does not speak what he does not know. He told Schnieper quite simply that he knew from an absolutely reliable source that the war would break out shortly. Moreover, through his contacts in Berlin, he would be in possession of information of an exceptional kind and he would like to put it at the disposal of the Allies.

There was a simple motive for this 'indiscretion'. Roessler knew that since the spring of that year Xavier

Schnieper had been serving as a soldier in a branch of Brigadier Masson's secret service. It had been Schnieper himself who had confided in him. He had been recruited on account of his journalistic work and also because he knew Germany well. He had often been asked if he knew anyone who might be useful to the service. Would Roessler allow him to put forward his name? The German émigré accepted with alacrity. So Schnieper introduced him to Major Hausamann's colleagues.

Hans Hausamann was a man of strong personality, who for this reason had often come into conflict with his superiors. He now owns a large photographic shop near Zürich railway-station. Before the war he had the reputation of belonging to the extreme Right. And yet there could have been few Swiss more hostile to Nazism than he was. Well before 1939, sensing the need to provide his country with secret eyes and ears, he had developed through his business a series of personal contacts throughout Europe, from Italy to Finland, which might if necessary be transformed into an information service. General Guisan had been very pleased to discover this private network. So the Swiss commander mobilised Hans Hausamann, but left him a considerable amount of autonomy. Moreover, he set Hausamann up with his own staff in the Villa Stutz, at Kastanienbaum, $8\frac{1}{2}$ kilometres south of Lucerne, on a tip of land that protrudes far into the Lake. This centre was given the name Bureau Ha.

If an up-to-date analysis of the political situation in Germany was required, it was the Bureau Ha that supplied it. If observation of German diplomats in Switzerland or protection of Swiss diplomats in Germany was needed, the Bureau was called in. And it was the Bureau Ha that sent Swiss agents into Germany.

Other branches of Brigadier Masson's service also sent spies into the Third Reich—generally dressed as privates or non-commissioned officers of the Wehrmacht and supplied with splendidly forged papers made in Berne, which allowed them into almost any garrison in Germany. Occasionally, these spies had extremely unfortunate experiences on their return to Switzerland—like the spy who managed to steal in Germany a *panzerfaust*, or bazooka, with its shell. On his return, he was arrested at the Col des Roches by Corporal Chevallier of the Swiss customs, who would not let him enter the country because he did not have an import-licence for his weapon. This produced a fine scandal which the customs service had the greatest difficulty in hushing up. But usually this kind of exploit was handled by the Bureau Ha. In the event of some unfortunate incident it was easier to disown them, since they were semi-clandestine in any case.

Xavier Schnieper presented his friend Roessler as an accomplished military specialist and praised his highly placed contacts in Germany. Roessler laid down his one, but important condition: he must never be questioned as to the sources of his information. Major Hausamann agreed. He knew too much about this kind of contact to insist. He would content himself with judging the recruit by his works. He was not to be disappointed.

The Berlin-Lucerne information service worked very well indeed. Suddenly on the night of Wednesday, August 23, 1939, the transmitter-receiver given to Roessler by T began to crackle. That morning, the chief of the Oberkommando of the Wehrmacht had held an extraordinary meeting. General Halder told them of the order given the night before by the Führer. "D Day against Poland fixed for Saturday 26."

In fact, after a last, desperate diplomatic manoeuvre by Britain and France, it was not until dawn on September 1 that the troops of the Wehrmacht crossed the Polish frontier *en masse* and converged on Warsaw from the north, south and west. On September 2 war was declared. *Werther* and *Olga* began their work of destroying the régime that was to last for a thousand years.

6

SWITZERLAND: A POPULATION
of under 5 million and an area of 41,344 square kilometres,
including 10,423 of uninhabitable rock and ice. A calm,
reserved, hard-working people, rearing the finest cows in
the world, and producing probably the best *Gruyère* and the
finest watches in the world. But their most precious asset
is their neutrality—and not just any kind of neutrality.

The *Journal de Genève* for Wednesday, August 30, 1939,
claimed that the 'voluntary' neutrality of Belgium and the
'independent' neutrality of Holland were not juridically the
same thing as the Confederation's 'total' neutrality, Switzerland being *more* neutral than the other neutral countries.

Switzerland believed that she had done everything
possible, secretly, to keep herself outside the bonfire that
Hitler was preparing for Europe. At the end of August 1939
she appeared in her most traditional rôle. A week before
the outbreak of the war, two symbolic events took place—
events with which Switzerland was most happy to identify
herself and which occupied the front pages of her newspapers. On Monday, August 21, the 33rd World Peace

Conference was solemnly opened in Zürich. The whole of Europe, except Germany, Italy and Spain, was represented. The next day, the International Red Cross, that owed so much to Switzerland, celebrated its 75th anniversary in Geneva.

In this stormy, rainy holiday month—at Basle the firemen were called out seven hundred times on the Monday to pump out flooded cellars—all the hotels were full. There had never been so many British and French tourists. The national exhibition in Zürich was enjoying an immense success. On the previous day, Sunday, August 20, the seven millionth visitor passed through the turnstiles. Everything helped to hide the spectre at the feast. Two cinemas, however, offered programmes that reflected the oncoming drama. In Geneva, the Cinébref announced 'Danzig, the only newsreel taken in the Free City.' And in Lausanne the Moderne-Cinéma was presenting a documentary on 'The Maginot Line, the most amazing defensive creation of modern times.' But the takings were far greater at the Rex, with Fernandel in *Raphael le Tatoué*, and at the ABC, with Raimu in *Monsieur Bretonneau*.

However, on Thursday, August 24, 1939, the Federal Council took a secret census of Swiss industry—an action of the greatest importance, since it was intended to provide the essential basis for its commercial policy, particularly for its war economy. The same day, just as secretly, the Swiss postal department, with the agreement of the Federal police, seized hundreds of letters intended for Germany. They contained anti-Nazi propaganda of British origin. On the eve of the war, the Confederation could not afford to give Hitler the slightest pretext to question Swiss neutrality.

An indication that the war was not far off occurred the following day, Friday, August 25. The United Kingdom ambassador in Berne warned all British subjects wishing to leave Switzerland that they should do so that same night. After which time it seemed highly probable that the normal services of the international railways would be suspended.

The next day, August 26, the Federal Council held an

extraordinary meeting in Berne. The German Minister in Berne had just confirmed that the Reich would respect the neutrality of Switzerland in the event of war. Giuseppe Motta, head of the Political Department, emphasised that this in no way dispensed Switzerland from the duty to make it possible to defend that neutrality if necessary. It was no more than the other neutrals, Belgium, the Netherlands and Luxembourg had done after receiving similar assurances from Germany. Herr Minger, head of the Military Department, insisted that Switzerland must be ready to defend her frontiers at the first sign of danger. All the Federal councillors were asked not to leave Berne, so that they might be consulted on the spot if the need arose.

They did not have to wait long. At 3 pm Monday, August 28, the councillors filed once more into the Federal Palace. At the same time a significant event took place at Chiasso, a town on the Italian frontier, near Lake Como. Sixty-two Polish Jews, who had come to attend the Zionist Conference in Geneva, were on their way home via Italy— thus avoiding Austria or Germany. Insulted and stoned by Italian fascists they stood huddled together in the Chiasso customs office, awaiting the return of their representative who had gone to ask for the help of the Swiss authorities of the canton of the Ticino.

At 5 am the next day, Switzerland mobilised its frontier troops. By press and radio, M. Philippe Etter, the President of the Confederation, instructed all men who had the red form in their army-books, to go without delay to the meeting-places arranged. The rest of the population were asked to keep calm.

"Do not panic. I would particularly ask you to refrain from spreading false rumours, from making unnecessary purchases of food and from sudden withdrawals of money from the banks. All steps have been taken to guarantee adequate food supplies and the free circulation of money. Tomorrow, Wednesday, August 30, at 5 pm, the Federal Assembly will elect a general. I repeat: all necessary steps have been taken."

What stuck in the minds of most of the President's listeners were the words, "The Federal Assembly will elect a general." For them, this was sure proof that war would break out very shortly. For the Swiss Army, a family army —each soldier keeps his rifle, ammunition and other equipment at home—has no general in peace-time. According to article 89, chapter 3, of the Constitution, the Assembly entrusts the command of this army to an officer elected for the purpose when the Confederation's neutrality is threatened. There had been General Dufour in 1859, at the time of the war between Italy and Austria; General Herzog in 1870; General Ulrich Wille in 1914. The fourth Swiss general was to be Henri Guisan. Switzerland had been expecting the outbreak of war for so long now that Colonel Guisan had known for some months that he would be offered the post.

On Wednesday, August 30, Henri Guisan, a very young-looking sixty-five, was duly elected general with 204 votes against 21 for his opponent, Colonel Borel. There were two abstentions—those of the Communist councillors, Bodeman and Humbert. Guisan took the oath of allegiance to the Confederation and swore to defend, with the troops under his command, the honour, independence and neutrality of his country.

It was the same oath that Ulrich Wille had taken in 1914. There the resemblance between the two men ends. Wille was a cautious man who kept well within his terms of reference. Guisan did not hesitate to go beyond them if he considered that it was for the good of his country. Under Wille, Switzerland had been pro-German; under Guisan it was to play, as best it could, the Allies' game. Wille was cold and forbidding; Henri Guisan was to become the most popular citizen in the Confederation.

The day before the general mobilisation, Giuseppe Motta, head of the Political Department, received in turn the representatives of the future belligerents. They assured him that the Confederation's territory and neutrality would be respected. Signor Tamaro, the Italian ambassador, had even gone so far as to say that Italy's trans-alpine ports and roads would be open for Swiss traffic. All that was needed was for the two governments to settle the 'details' of such an agreement. Motta thanked the ambassador for what seemed a very generous offer, but, secretly, it gave him no pleasure at all. It could not be as simple as Tamaro made out, for Switzerland was entering a time of compromises, overt commitments and secret agreements.

On Saturday, September 2, the day of the mobilisation, armoured lorries made a tour of the Swiss banks. The safes were emptied and the contents taken to a kind of Ali Baba's cave in the middle of the Alps. Switzerland was quick to protect one of its chief assets—the fortunes of others.

At dawn, that same Saturday, 400,000 men took up their positions around the country's frontiers. On the orders of the Federal Council, Henri Guisan had had to set up his headquarters in a hotel, the Bellevue, 3 Kochergasse, in Berne—to be nearer the Federal palace. It was there, on the third floor, that General Wille set up his headquarters in 1914. Wille may have felt at home there. Certainly Guisan didn't. He insisted on moving, and went first to Spiez, then to Gumligen, then to Interlaken, finally to Jegenstorf.

The Swiss upper class, which always tended to be pro-German, was not slow to claim that Guisan travelled around a great deal more than necessary, that too many little girls came to bring him flowers and murmur compliments, that he tended to incite the adulation of the people, to the detriment of his military duties. It was even pointed out that he had totally eclipsed the President of the Confederation in the people's affections. But it was not to the office, but to the man that the Swiss were drawn. The Swiss felt vaguely that Guisan was doing more for the defence of their country than any of his predecessors and that they would be safe in his hands. But Guisan did not always stop to receive the acclamations of the crowd—his time was extremely limited. For, contrary to what some people believed, he never stopped working on behalf of his army and slept no more than five hours a night.

When he took charge of Switzerland's defence, he had at his disposal a very vulnerable army which, he is said to have remarked, could not hold out longer than a week against attack: 600 rounds of ammunition per man, forty-four anti-aircraft guns, 835 anti-tank guns, 121 reconnaissance planes and eighty-six fighters, including a few Messerschmitts, but most of which were old D27s, nicknamed 'flying coffins'. He intended to change all that. He wanted to entrench the Swiss army in fortresses to be dug out of the Alps, and mountain-passes and tunnels were to be blocked. Stocks of food and ammunition had to be organised. He wanted to build up an army that could stave off an aggressor for two years. This was to act as a guarantee, at least as a front, to his country's often quoted 'total' neutrality.

Secretly, Henri Guisan carried his plans much further. He was well aware that a German émigré of exceptional value had settled in Lucerne and had offered his services to Major Hans Hausamann's Bureau Ha, in which he took a particular interest. Guisan felt that before long such a collaboration would present very serious problems of conscience. But he decided to ignore them and stifle his scruples. For him, too, it was absolutely vital that Nazi Germany should lose the war.

7

MOST ESPIONAGE CASES ARE
based upon a single, often quite crucial, but none the less
isolated event of short duration. The master-stroke of
Richard Sorge, for example, was the acquisition of information that proved Japan would not attack the Soviet Union.
It enabled Stalin to leave Siberia virtually undefended and
to throw his best divisions against Hitler without fear of
attack from the East. The enormous value of Rudolf
Roessler and his ten collaborators of the *Viking Line*, as
the Swiss named them, was based on a body of information
just as sensational as that of Richard Sorge, but which
lasted for *four years*.

The quantity of information communicated by these
German resisters to the Swiss—quite apart from the information they supplied later to others, in even larger quantities
—amounts to twelve thousand closely typed pages, the
equivalent of about forty average-length books.

Almost every day, Roessler arrived at the Villa Stutz, at
Kastanienbaum, with a pile of documents in a brief-case.
From the time he was engaged by the Swiss, military experts

were able, with the information supplied by *Werther* and *Olga*, to reconstruct in the greatest detail, the movements and strategy of the Wehrmacht.

It might be said, without fear of contradiction, that it was these eleven men, ten of whom remained unknown to Brigadier Roger Masson, that were responsible for the reputation of the Swiss secret service. It was they, in fact, who won the admiration of Sir Alexander Cadogan, head of the British Intelligence Service, and of General Donovan, the head of the OSS (Office of Strategic Service), the American espionage organisation—though these two men were unaware of whom exactly they were admiring.

In November 1942, Allen Dulles, General Donovan's special envoy in Switzerland, and future head of the famous CIA, took up residence in an anonymous-looking house in the Herrengasse in Zürich. Dulles made no secret of the purpose of his mission in Switzerland: to make contact with the German opposition to the Führer and work out what could be done to overthrow Nazism. He was the first among the Allies to sense the importance of those Swiss contacts who appeared to be so close to Hitler. These men would be admirably suited to help him achieve his end.

He had the Villa Stutz watched, and Roessler followed, but in vain. He then turned to another branch of the German opposition, that of the German vice-consul in Zürich, Hans Bernd Gisevius, a friend of Admiral Canaris, head of the Abwehr, who was later to take part in the abortive attempt on Hitler's life on July 20, 1944. Roger Masson soon recovered from his initial surprise at the American's rather overt and unconventional methods and, realising that they were doomed to failure, let him go his own way. What Dulles was trying to do in the open, Masson, thanks to Roessler, had long been doing in secret.

The head of Swiss Intelligence was faced with a serious problem of conscience when he learnt that an agent as well informed as Roessler had offered his services to Switzerland. In the wealth of information promised by this man it was obvious that very little would be of direct concern to Switzerland, a very minor objective for German expansionism. On the other hand, it was just as obvious that western Europe would be attacked. But Masson could not compromise the future of the Confederation by officially warning the diplomatic representatives of these countries whenever some information concerning them reached him. Yet his pro-Ally feelings obliged him to try and help them. He must discover an effective means of doing this without involving Switzerland, at least overtly.

It was Hans Hausamann who found a temporary solution to the problem. In fact, it was to last until 1944. Quite by chance a foreigner—said to be the Canadian uncle of Hausamann's wife and whom they nicknamed 'Uncle Tom' —was at the Villa Stutz, when Rudolf Roessler brought some information that would be of great service to the Allies. This man, in fact, was Czech, a Colonel Sedlacek; thus the worst accusation that could be levelled at Switzerland was that it had behaved 'frivolously' or 'imprudently'.

Soon after the opening of the Wehrmacht's campaign in Poland, Roessler had become a sufficiently accomplished wireless-operator, having absorbed well the lessons of his friend, Christian Schneider. Schneider asked no questions. He claimed to be a communist and although he did not share Roessler's ideas he knew that it was not to help the Nazis that he had obtained the transmitter.

The first news transmitted by Roessler concerned the terror exercised by the Nazis. On September 23, 1939, he arrived at the Villa Stutz overcome with emotion. He brought with him a copy of a plan that Heydrich had issued to the Army High Command two days before:

"The Third Reich will not rebuild Poland. As soon as the conquest has been completed, the aristocracy and the clergy must be exterminated. The people must be kept at a very low standard of living. They will thus provide cheap slaves. The Jews will be grouped into the towns where they will remain easily accessible. The *final solution*, Heydrich states, will take some time to be worked out and must be kept strictly secret."

86

For the officers of the Wehrmacht—and for those Swiss who learnt of this message—there could be no doubt as to the meaning of the phrase 'final solution'. It meant extermination. These orders, which had been inspired directly by the Führer, were to be carried out by Hans Frank, who had been appointed Governor-General of Poland.

"It is a difficult matter," he was later to admit, "to shoot or poison three and a half million Polish Jews, but we will be able to take the necessary steps to bring about their annihilation."

His words were to prove true enough.

Colonel Sedlacek was at the Villa Stutz when Roessler sent news that the Wehrmacht was preparing to attack Holland, Belgium and north-eastern France. It was October 13, 1939. Three days before, Hitler had called a meeting of his generals. He was very annoyed because Halder and Brauchitsch had declared that it would take several months to repair the damage done to the tank units by the Polish campaign. The Führer had shouted and banged his fist on his desk in the Chancellery.

"Time is on the enemy's side!" he shouted. "Preparations must be speeded up for an offensive through Luxembourg, Belgium and Holland. We must do the worst possible damage to the French Army and gain as much ground as possible. I am asking the commanders-in-chief to supply me with detailed reports of their plans as soon as possible. A war of position, as in 1914-18, must be avoided. The armoured divisions will be used for the crucial thrusts. The attack on Holland and Belgium will take place on November 12."

'Uncle Tom' went at once to inform the British Embassy. The Dutch and the Belgians were also told. On November 7 Roessler announced that the offensive had been postponed. The conflict between Hitler and his generals had not been resolved. During the autumn and winter of 1939-40, there were fourteen such decisions and postponements. Each time, Rudolf Roessler warned the Swiss and the Allies were told.

On November 23, 1939, the Führer called a new meeting of his generals in the Chancellery. This time, in addition to the offensive to the West, with which he was concerned above everything else, Hitler mentioned the possibility of a war on two fronts—a nightmare for any military leader. He spoke for the first time of an attack on Russia, despite the treaty that bound Germany to the Soviet Union. To justify this extension of the conflict, he attributed his own motives to the Soviet Union, thus disguising his own personal objectives:

"Treaties," he declared, "are respected as long as they serve a particular interest. Russia will respect ours only as long as she considers it to be to her own advantage. . . . She still has very far-reaching aims, notably the strengthening of her position in the Baltic. The moment seems to be a judicious one."

This information, brought by Roessler, disturbed the Swiss. Helping the western Allies flattered their dignity, their instinctive solidarity with a world like their own. But what could they do with this message? Despite the hospitality they had formerly accorded to a few of the Russian revolutionary leaders, they had a poor opinion of the communist régime. Moreover, the Soviet Union was not yet at war with Nazi Germany. Worse still, she could even be regarded as Germany's accomplice, since the petrol used by the Wehrmacht in Poland came from Baku, and the corn consumed by these same German soldiers from the Ukraine. To offer help to the Russians would therefore be a betrayal.

After some reflection, the Swiss decided to postpone any decision of this kind. So the Bureau Ha simply kept Roessler's message to themselves—and Roessler supported their decision. At this stage, he was still full of confidence. He did not yet realise that the West would take no account of the exceptional value of his information.

A flood of communications was to follow. *Werther* and *Olga* omitted none of the Führer's plans and their application by the OKW. In January 1940 and throughout February, as Hitler moved on to the preparations for the invasion of

Norway, the Bureau Ha was kept informed. From February 26, Masson's men had complete details of the coming invasion.

On March 1 Hitler addressed a directive to his generals concerning the future occupation of Denmark—an operation that was to be linked to General Falkendorf's invasion of Norway. Both operations, claimed Hitler, would prevent Britain getting a foothold in Scandinavia and the Baltic. They would also guarantee Sweden's ore resources, which had been put at Germany's disposal. A week later the Bureau Ha received the main contents of this directive.

Long before the Wehrmacht could put their plans against Scandinavia into practice, Denmark and Norway had been tipped off by the Swiss. None the less, both countries were 'surprised'. On the evening of April 8, the King of Denmark went to the Royal Theatre, in spite of the fact that Copenhagen had learnt of the torpedoing of a German troop-ship by a Polish submarine south of Norway, and that a fleet of the Kriegsmarine was making for its ports. That day, the Norwegian cabinet seemed equally strangely inactive, even when several ships had been sighted moving towards the Norwegian coast.

On March 30, 1940, and again on April 3, 1940, Colonel J. G. Sas, Dutch military attaché in Berlin, had been warned by the Swiss military attaché of the fate that awaited Denmark. Curiously enough, Colonel Oster, an adjutant of Admiral Canaris, the head of the Abwehr, who was on close personal terms with Sas, also warned him of the danger. Sas immediately informed Captain Kjölsen, the Danish naval attaché. But the Danish government failed to act on the information, even though it was confirmed by two sources.

On March 25, 1940, on the basis of information from the Bureau Ha, the Norwegian government was also warned, through its legation in Berne, of the threat to its country. The Swiss agent emphasised the extreme reliability of the information—but to no avail. He was believed no more than his predecessors. Again, another source—this time Swedish, the military attaché in Berlin in fact—confirmed the news on April 5, in vain. The German plan, *Weserübung*, succeeded perfectly!

This tragic episode was typical of the strange reactions of the European high commands and the democratic governments of the period. Unaccustomed to the participation of intelligence services in the conduct of battles, they reacted with instinctive mistrust—and it was this reaction that drove them straight into catastrophe. Neither Belgium, Holland, nor France escaped the catastrophe—and for the same reason. Like Denmark and Norway they were given ample warning from secret agents, but refused to listen.

In fact, astonished, but in no way discouraged by the indecision of the Danish and Norwegian leaders who had played so well into Hitler's hands, Rudolf Roessler persevered, as a flood of alarming information reached him from Maybach camp at Zossen.

He had long known that Belgium, the Netherlands and France were next on the list for attack. The final version of the 'yellow plan' against the West, the plan worked out by General Erich von Manstein, appeared on February 27, 1940. On March 10, General Delvoie, the Belgian military attaché in Paris, acting on orders from his government, which had been warned by the Swiss (that is, by Roessler), passed on to the French High Command the main outlines of the plan.

What was this 'yellow plan'? An offensive on the Meuse, between Charleville and Sedan and a breakthrough across the Ardennes, while the main body of the Wehrmacht would hold down the mass of French, Belgian and British forces on the west of the front, on the Belgian frontier. The panzers of General Hermann Hoth and General Heinz Guderian were to make the intended attack on the Sedan Gap, then swivel in a gigantic curve in the direction of the lower Somme, with the intention of reaching the sea, thus trapping most of the Allied army. General Thomas had made provision for only three weeks' supplies of ammunition and fuel.

But on March 10, the French High Command were in possession of the full details of the plan!

On May 1, Roessler received a brief message from *Werther*:

"Attack May 10 in the Sedan Gap. Yellow plan still holds. Fifty divisions massed along the Belgian and Dutch frontiers. Guderian and Hoth ready to charge on Sedan."

A few days before, the French military attaché in Berne, secretly alerted by a messenger from the Bureau Ha, Colonel Sedlacek, 'Uncle Tom', telegraphed at once to Paris: "German attack will probably take place May 10. It will be directed against Sedan."

It was to be hoped that this time the Allied high commands would not be taken by surprise, as those of Denmark and Norway had been, and that they would be ready for the Wehrmacht and position the equipment necessary to tear into the oncoming 136 German divisions. This was all the more to be hoped as on the same day, General Gauché, head of the Deuxième Bureau, and Colonel Rivet, head of the Cinquième Bureau, never stopped sending the numerous confirmations they had received from Switzerland to the French government and High Command—on May 4, 6 and 8, etc.

On May 10, at dawn, the Wehrmacht attacked. No one expected it at the point where it made its main thrust, at the places indicated by *Werther*. On May 13, Sedan fell. Three days later, Guderian's tanks were rolling, a hundred kilometres to the west of Sedan, across open countryside, with no opposition in sight. On May 24, the Allies were encircled, 'the gigantic curve' was over. The whole operation had been conducted with perfect rigour—for German land forces were not noted for their powers of improvisation. The three armies, the Belgian, British and French, endured a terrible bombardment within a small triangle of ground. The only hope of escape for some was by sea from Dunkerk.

Strategists may argue at leisure about the development of this campaign of 1939-40, comparing figures and hypothetical tactics. But they will find no valid explanation for this tragic fact: the French and British High Commands made no use of the extraordinary information that had been communicated to them, always well in advance, to turn events in their own favour.

These high commands were very largely responsible for the defeat of 1940. They cannot seek to evade that responsibility. They will never be able to exculpate themselves from the accusations that can be made against them for their failure at that time. Through their fault, Europe fell under German occupation and millions of human beings were sacrificed to the madness of the Nazis.

The collapse of the Allies, due very largely to the incredulity of the military high commands in the secret struggle that was being waged in their support, stupefied Rudolf Roessler. Stupefaction was followed by bitterness. From his home at Wesemlin, where his transmitter-receiver was hidden, he alerted his friends. They were to stop sending documents and limit themselves to weekly interchanges. It was pointless for *Werther* and *Olga* to expose themselves to danger when no one took the slightest notice of what they were being offered.

General Guisan, too, was now undergoing a certain amount of anxiety. Although the military leader of a neutral country, he, too, like Roessler, had been trying to help the Allies. Convinced of an early Allied victory, he had even been imprudent enough to sign a secret military convention with France, which might be used against the Confederation if it were to fall into the hands of the Germans. The very future of Switzerland might be in jeopardy. It was at this point that Guisan conceived a line of national defence. It was more than ever necessary to maintain the Berlin-Lucerne contact that Masson and Hausamann regarded so highly and of which they were so proud. In the event of Hitler deciding on an invasion of Swiss territory, Guisan would know about it sufficiently well in advance to organise his last desperate resistance.

For the Swiss general had never under-estimated the importance of the secret service. It might even be said that it formed one of the basic components of his strategy. Masson himself, or one of his assistants, was always present at every meeting of the High Command—which was the case in hardly any country in the world. Guisan was unique in that he always paid particular attention to information that came from his secret service. Ignorant of the causes of the temporary interruption in activity between Roessler and the Bureau Ha, and even that there was such an interruption, Xavier Schnieper was instructed to ask his German friend to come urgently to the Villa Stutz.

Hausamann managed to find the right words for the occasion:

"Switzerland is in danger and the Nazis are drunk with victory, but all is not yet lost. A resistance movement has begun in Norway and before long a similar movement will begin in France. On June 18, General de Gaulle made an appeal from London. Great Britain will not give in. We must therefore continue our work. It is Roessler's duty to do so. The Confederation opened its frontiers to him when misfortune struck his country. He, in turn, should help them in the trials that lie ahead."

Only too happy to serve, Rudolf Roessler immediately alerted his friends in Berlin. They were not to give up. The struggle must begin again. Top priority was to be given to any information which might be of value to Switzerland.

In mid-July 1940 there was a tense situation on the western frontier between Saint-Louis and Gex. Masson's own agents had discovered six German divisions, two of mountain-troops, encamped near the border and ready to attack. They also mentioned border patrols, the laying of telephone cable, and German espionage activity around Swiss installations in the area. Were these indications of a forthcoming surprise attack? Roessler asked Berlin. On July 18, less than twenty-four hours after his request, he received a full reply. There was nothing to fear for the moment. The Oberkommando of the Wehrmacht was too preoccupied with the problems presented by a possible invasion of Britain, the

'Otarie plan', for it to have any time to give to Switzerland.

Reassured for the present and wishing to make full use of Roessler's services, the Swiss now asked him whether, in addition to his other work, he would take on another job. They wanted him to sift and evaluate the mass of information they received. Most of the work of their secret service consisted simply in the amassing of information, but this information had then to be interpreted, given its relative importance and fitted in to a total synthesis.

This work required a clear, ordered, mathematical mind, together with considerable military knowledge and a flair for geo-politics. Rudolf Roessler was perfectly suited to such a job. Moreover, his nationality and intellectual training made him particularly able to guess how a fellow-German reacted to or tackled a particular problem. Roessler agreed.

Nevertheless, he in no way neglected the mission he was carrying out for *Werther* and *Olga*. On August 3, 1940, he communicated an important message to the Swiss centre at Lucerne which he had received only an hour before. On July 31 Hitler had informed his High Command of his irrevocable decision to attack Russia. His statement showed that his own plans of aggression had been ready for a long time:

"I am convinced that Britain's determination to continue the struggle is based upon the expected support of the USSR. Strange things are taking place on the other side of the Channel. Yesterday, the British were laid low. Now they are once more on their feet. It is enough that Russia, anxious on account of our conquests in the West, should let it be understood that she would not view with favour any further development of German power for the British to cling like drowning men to the hope of a complete reversal of the situation within a few months. If we crush Russia, Britain's last plank of hope will sink with her. And Germany will become the mistress of Europe, including the Balkans. For these reasons Russia must be liquidated. The attack will take place in the spring of 1941.

"We shall launch two offensives at once—one in the south, in the direction of Kiev and the Dnieper, the other in the north, through the Baltic States, towards Moscow. There the two armies will link up. Then, if necessary, a special operation will be made to give us the Baku oil-fields. One hundred and twenty divisions will be allocated to this front. Sixty will be enough in the West. The offensive will last five months and begin in March 1941 . . ."

This information was a great consolation for the Swiss, for if war was to break out between Germany and Russia, the Reich would have no troops left to invade the Confederation. But at the same time the information was a cause of embarrassment. Not knowing what to make of it, the Swiss were prepared to keep it to themselves.

"But one day, you will have to decide to communicate this news to the Russians," Roessler remarked to Hausamann. "You know very well that more information of this kind will be forthcoming and in ever larger quantities. I must remember that my objective, and that of the men I represent, is the death of Nazism. We are ready to help whoever will do most to achieve that end, whatever their nationality."

"But Germany and Russia are not at war yet," Major Hausamann interrupted. "And there is nothing to show such an anti-Nazi determination on the part of the Russians. In any case, we shall never communicate with them."

"Am I to understand that *I* shall be allowed to warn them?"

Hausamann was astute enough not to reply.

From that August of 1940, while continuing to supply the Swiss with information on the movements of German troops within the Reich, and analysing this information, Roessler was studying ways of warning the Russians. Time was running short. Among the avalanche of details that poured out of the OKW offices, there were notes that indicated in ever greater detail that preparations for the invasion of the Soviet Union were going ahead.

On December 5, 1940, Generals Halder and Brauchitsch

submitted to the Führer the 'Otto plan', the details of the attack worked out by the High Command. Moscow, it suggested, was not an important objective. The Red Army would be pushed back into the Pripet Marshes from the north and the south. It would be encircled and destroyed. Rumania and Finland would share in the spoils—and the two attacks launched from these countries. They would also supply support troops for the Wehrmacht. At the head of the Finnish troops, General Dietl's mountain troops would advance on Petsamo in Lapland and occupy the Arctic ports. This division would have to be transferred from Narvik to Finland through Sweden, which had just agreed to this.

Hitler accepted the 'Otto plan' enthusiastically. He put some finishing touches to it, re-named it 'Operation Barbarossa' and read it out to his generals on December 18, 1940. The preliminaries of the operation were to be completed by May 15 the following year. This perfect plan was to remain unaltered. To preserve the maximum possible secrecy, Hitler ordered that only nine copies should be made of it. One was distributed to each of the armed forces: the Wehrmacht, the Luftwaffe and the Kriegsmarine. The other six were to remain at Maybach camp, the OKW headquarters.

A week later, just after Christmas, Rudolf Roessler received the longest message so far. It was in eight instalments spread over a period of forty-eight hours. It took twelve hours to decipher. It was a real bombshell—nothing less than a complete copy of 'Operation Barbarossa'. This was the biggest fish so far caught by his friends. Confronted with this document, Roessler felt troubled. He could well imagine the difficulties his friends must be encountering. Even if they were able to see important plans in the normal course of their work, it was also necessary to get hold of them, secretly. They were obviously taking ever greater risks. And he did not know what to do with the results!

He had tried in vain to find a way of warning the

Walter Schellenberg

Reinhard Heydrich

Rudolf Roessler

Roger Masson

Villa Stutz, at Kastanienbaum, near Lucerne, the headquarters of the Bureau Ha

A simple plaque in the Swiss cemetery at Kriens marks the grave of the greatest resistance worker of the Second World War

La F.A.O.
sera-t-elle dirigée par un Suisse ?

(C.P.S.) — Nous croyons savoir que le Conseil fédéral s'occupera dans une de ses prochaines séances de la succession à la direction générale de l'Organisation internationale de l'agriculture (Food and Agricultur Organization F.A.O.) On sait que la plus haute partie de cette section technique de l'O.N.U. depuis la création de celle-ci et qu'elle y est représentée par le professeur F. T. Wahlen, auteur du fameux plan d'extension des cultures pendant la guerre. Depuis trois ans, M. Wahlen fait partie de l'administration de cette organisation en qualité de chef de la division de l'agriculture.

A la suite du départ du directeur général actuel de la F.A.O., l'Américain Norris E. Dodd, atteint par la limite d'âge, l'assemblée générale convoquée pour la fin du mois à Rome aura à régler la succession. En principe chaque gouvernement membre de la F.A.O. est libre de proposer un de ses concitoyens pour l'un des postes d'administration de la F.A.O. M. Wahlen étant un expert en matière agricole et un spécialiste de la F.A.O. quoi de plus naturel que le Conseil fédéral présente sa candidature au poste de directeur de l'organisation. Le Conseil fédéral désignera par la même occasion la délégation suisse à l'assemblée générale.

Le jugement
contre Roessler et Schnieper

(C.P.S.) — La Cour pénale fédérale, siégeant à Lucerne, a rendu jeudi matin son jugement dans l'affaire des espions Roessler et Schnieper. Les deux accusés sont reconnus coupables d'un service de renseignements pour un Etat étranger au préjudice d'un autre Etat étranger et condamné à une peine d'emprisonnement d'une année pour Roessler et de neuf mois pour Schnieper, sous déduction de la préventive. Comme les deux condamnés ont déjà subi une détention de 212 jours pendant la durée de l'instruction, Roessler devra encore purger quatre mois et Schnieper un mois.

Le tribunal n'a pas donné suite à la demande d'expulsion introduite par le représentant du Ministère public contre Roessler. Dans ses considérants, il relève que ce dernier a effectivement abusé du droit d'asile suisse, mais qu'il faut considérer qu'il est établi depuis vingt ans dans notre pays et qu'il nous a rendu de précieux services durant la guerre. D'autre part, le condamné étant apatride, une peine de bannissement aurait eu pour lui des conséquences très dures.

LAUSANNE, *au jour le jour*

The ' Roessler Affair ' of 1953

Le procès intenté pour service de renseignements au profit d'un pays étranger à Rudolf Roessler, éditeur, 58 ans, et Xaver Schnieper, journaliste, 43 ans, s'est ouvert à Lucerne devant le Tribunal pénal fédéral, présidé par Me Corrodi, juge fédéral. Les accusés ont fait de l'espionnage en faveur de la Tchécoslovaquie, contre la République fédérale allemande, les Etats-Unis, l'Angleterre, la France et le Danemark. Notre photo: Schnieper (à gauche) et Roessler arrivent devant la maison lucernoise où a lieu le procès.

Russians by means of a third party. There remained only one solution, which he had so far rejected because it would compel him to deal with the communists—his friend Christian Schneider, the man who had helped him to assemble his transmitter-receiver and taught him Morse. Roessler knew Schneider's opinions only too well, having argued against them on the occasion of the signing of the German-Soviet pact. He invited his fellow-countryman to lunch. During the meal in a Lucerne restaurant, the Unter der Egg, on the banks of the Reuss, not far from his office, he asked Schneider point-blank: "Do you know how I could talk to the Russians?"

"Just talk?" Schneider asked, surprised.

Roessler decided not to beat about the bush.

"I am not joking, Christian. I have information in my hands that is too hot to hold. It could be of the greatest use to the Soviet Union. If they want to pay for it they can do so later. I shall have more, believe me. I am quite willing to collaborate—though I don't care for the word—for nothing."

Schneider pondered for a time.

"If you don't make them pay you," he said at last, "they'll take you for an *agent-provocateur*. I know them. Is it really important information?"

Roessler decided to be frank.

"It's about the war. The Germans want to invade Russia."

"Are you sure of your source?" Schneider asked incredulously.

"Absolutely. You remember my wireless-set? I have friends in Germany. They could hardly be better placed. I lay down only one condition on my co-operation. My friends run enough risks as it is. The Russians must never try to find out who they are."

Christian Schneider rose and murmured doubtfully:

"It is certain that that would be the most difficult thing for Moscow to accept. I'll see you in a fortnight."

Two weeks later, Schneider called at the Vita Nova

Verlag in Lucerne. The two men went out and talked as they strolled down to the Reuss.

The anonymity clause had not helped matters. The Russians still knew nothing about the matter, but in Geneva there was a Soviet information cell. Schneider worked for this cell. Without mentioning him by name, he had spoken of Roessler to the head of this group, who did not seem very impressed. He was willing to give the matter a try, but he could not answer for the reactions of the 'Centre', the organisation in Moscow that directed the activities of all the 'delegations' abroad. For security reasons, Roessler was never to meet the Soviet official responsible in Switzerland, nor even know his name. Similarly, Geneva would know nothing of Roessler.

Between Geneva and Lucerne there would be two 'cut-outs', that is, two people who would hand on Roessler's information. If the Swiss—or the Germans—arrested them, neither the cell in Geneva nor Roessler should suffer. For these intermediaries always have a capsule containing cyanide concealed on their persons which they swallow if the situation becomes serious enough.

The first 'cut-out' was to be Schneider himself, and the second a woman friend of his; if anything happened to him she was to take his place as the first intermediary. She was called Rachel Duebendorfer, and like himself she was employed by the International Labour Office. She lived in Geneva with her daughter Tamara. Although of Balkan origin she had a Swiss passport—just before the war she had gone through a 'white' marriage with a Swiss. This was a fairly common practice at the time and one that was highly profitable to a number of Swiss citizens who sold their names—and the security that they brought with them. In actual fact, Rachel Duebenforfer was living with her lover, Paul Boetcher, an ex-German minister—also an émigré and a communist.

"Is everything clear, then?" Schneider asked. "You give me your information, I pass it on to Rachel, who takes it to Geneva. Two more things! If Moscow accepts your co-operation, you will be paid. Secondly, you must change your name. We all have pseudonyms. I'm 'Taylor', Rachel is 'Sissi' and you will be known as 'Lucy'."

Thus, in the spring of 1941, Rudolf Roessler—a liberal, Protestant German from a respectable, conservative, upper middle-class Bavarian background, a man who, despite his emigration, had retained the class-consciousness of his caste, became, out of hatred of Nazism, a Soviet secret agent. He did so with the blessing of the Bureau Ha and Masson, who agreed on condition that he continued to work for Switzerland and supply information which would be useful to the western Allies.

Fate, which played so large a rôle throughout this extraordinary affair, was soon to take a hand once more in a strangely amusing way. Roessler, though frail in appearance, had unbounded vitality and slept no more than three hours a night. In spite of all his various secret activities, he could not prevent himself from continuing with his writing —as always, under his pseudonym, R. A. Hermes. At the beginning of 1941, he published a remarkable analysis of the strategy of the Wehrmacht, *Die Kriegsschauplätze und die Bedingungen der Kriegsführung* (Theatres of War and the Conditions for their Conduct)—a work of ninety closely printed pages. As illustrations for this little book, he needed twelve specially drawn maps showing the various movements of the German Army.

So he called on the services of the best geographical firm in Switzerland, the Géo-Presse in Geneva. The head of this company came to Lucerne personally to discuss Roessler's sketches with him. This man never knew that he had opposite him the most important Soviet spy in the world. And Roessler did not know that this thick-set, rather corpulent figure, who spoke six languages, who was so adept at translating his ideas into concrete form, was the head of the Russian spy network in Switzerland, Alexander Rado, his new boss.

8

MORE THAN ANY OF THE
traditional 'covers' used by spies, it was his natural gaiety
that protected Alexander Radolfi, known as 'Rado' to his
friends. It was difficult to imagine this happy extravert
engaged in plotting and spying—it seemed far more likely
he would be chasing a girl or savouring a good meal. Yet
this Hungarian was a master-spy, a colonel of the Red Army
trained in a very special school, Sekhjodnya, the training
centre of the Soviet espionage service outside Moscow.
Before that Rado had worked for the Comintern, fomenting
revolutions throughout Europe—in his own country, in
Czechoslovakia, Poland and Germany, where he met his
wife Helene. In 1936, the MGB, the Ministry of State
Security, the 'Centre' as it was known familiarly to Soviet
spies, appointed him resident-director in Switzerland.

Contrary to the meaning of the term, a resident never
lived in the territory for which he was responsible. He
operated from a neighbouring country, whose laws he was
careful not to contravene, so that he could be left completely
in peace. His agents did the actual espionage work in the

country concerned, but he alone held possession of the pre-arranged codes and transmitted the news to the 'Centre'. Living in the shelter of Geneva, Alexander Rado's responsibility was Germany.

In 1939, shortly before the outbreak of war, he had hardly begun to attack. He had received strict instructions to build up a large network before attempting any operations of importance—and to compartment it by means of 'cut-outs', according to the usual practice. If possible, the sources of information should not be connected with the Communist Party: in the event of a catastrophe such people should be disowned. On the other hand, the 'cut-outs' and the wireless-operators, vital elements to an espionage organisation, should belong to the Party: if they were captured they would be better equipped by their beliefs to defend themselves. If they were sufficiently well conditioned they would be capable of committing suicide should there be any danger that they would be forced to talk.

Lastly, Moscow instructed Rado that his network must always be ready to produce information, but until the order to do so was received he was to lie low and avoid the slightest suspicion of his secret activity. He had been given a good 'front'. He was head of a cartographical firm, the Géo-Presse, which specialised in the manufacture of globes and other maps needed by the press and the public.

This decision to keep Rado's network in a state of watchful inactivity was in fact a tactical ruse. It was to be kept as a reserve base and operate only if absolutely necessary. At this period, the USSR had no shortage of spies concerned with Germany. About twenty resident directors, assisted by three hundred agents, were dotted around Germany.

The prudence of this decision by the 'Centre' to use Rado's network only as a last resort was soon to be proved. The Abwehr and the Sicherheitsdienst were soon to wipe out almost completely the mass of Russian spies operating on German territory. One after another they were captured. A few of them went over to the German side. The rest were shot.

But in 1939, no one expected such a situation. Alexander Rado could take his time building up his network and concealing his striking force. In any case, a small Soviet cell was already operating against Germany from Switzerland. Since 1936, it had been directed by a woman known as 'Sonia'. Her real name was Ursula Schultz. Like her husband, Alfred, she was German. She had joined the Communist Party with the same fervour and enthusiasm that others enter holy orders. She had one aim—to serve the cause. For a long time all went well with this husband and wife team. They were spying together in China when the MGB purged its secret service of suspected Trotskyites, of which there appeared to be a great many. The Swiss post fell vacant and Ursula was sent to fill it. Shortly afterwards Alfred Schultz, at a loss without his wife, was arrested in Shanghai.

Ursula, alias 'Sonia', was a tall, slim, attractive young woman of about thirty-five in 1939. She was not lacking in intelligence—it was just that she had lost something of her faith. She had been deeply shaken by the German-Russian pact. How could these Soviet diplomats enjoy such apparently cordial relations with the Nazis, while the two countries were secretly locked in ruthless struggle?

She lived with her two children and a housekeeper in a large, rented villa at Caux, a summer and winter health-resort overlooking Montreux. She received a monthly salary of 1,000 Swiss francs, which enabled her to live in comfort. For some time she had been showing signs of a slackening of her usual vigilance. She had even set up in her garden the long aerial of her transmitter-receiver—the set itself she hid carelessly in a biscuit tin in her dining-room. She broadcast once a fortnight. She had only a few agents in Germany who supplied her at irregular intervals with information of a minor kind.

Rado was more active. Although he had not yet begun to operate, he had assembled by 1939 about fifty sources of information—primarily on Germany, but also on other countries. Foresight had always been one of his characteristics. Among his sources was a Lithuanian Jew, 'Isaac', who worked for the International Labour Office—a veritable nest of spies—and who supplied information on the League of Nations. 'Isaac' was doubled by a Frenchman, 'Brandt'. 'May' and 'Anna' were concerned with the rearmament of Italy. 'Lili of the Vatican' was a diplomat to the Holy See. Rado considered that the Soviet government might one day be grateful for his knowledge of the official and unofficial positions of the Church.

Rado's best source—until Roessler was taken on—was a certain very talented spy called Otto Pünter. 'Pakbo', as he was nicknamed, had set up his own small organisation, which he called *Rot*. It operated in South Germany and was composed of Germans who were hostile to Nazism. Incomparably less well placed, and also less effective, than Roessler's friends, this band of civilian notables supplied information that was occasionally of a military nature, but generally economic.

Otto Pünter was a Swiss ex-journalist who had belonged to the Swiss Social Democratic Party. He had been fighting fascism for a long time. During the Spanish Civil War he was in Italy where he supplied the Spanish Republicans with information concerning the transportation of arms by sea to General Franco. He began his espionage career on July 10, 1930, when he took part in the famous flight over Milan conceived by the Italian Randolfo Pacciardi, when thousands of anti-Mussolini tracts were dropped over the city. Such a past had attracted Alexander Rado. Having discovered, through an indiscretion on the part of the Swiss Communist Party, the address of Otto Pünter in Switzerland, Rado approached him and took him on.

The General Secretary of the Swiss Party, Léon Nicole, and his son, Pierre, helped Rado in the recruitment of his 'cut-outs'. All were members of the party, as Moscow wished. Most of them worked for the International Labour Office. The Nicoles had also sent Rado three agents: Margareta Bolli, an unmarried woman who lived at 8 bis rue Henri Mussard, in Geneva, and Edmond and Olga Hamel, who lived at 192 route de Florissant, also in Geneva. Margareta Bolli and Edmond Hamel became the wireless-operators of the network. Rado saw a great deal of these collaborators of his—particularly the young and pretty Margareta, who became his mistress.

But none of these people knew where Rado lived. Before returning home he always made several huge detours. No one must ever know that he lived at 113 rue de Lausanne. This long road stretched from the Gare de Cornavin, in Geneva, to the Parc Mon-Repos, which overlooked Lake Leman.

This, then, was the situation in this powerful, 'inactive' organisation, when it was suddenly brought to life by the little man from Kaufbeuren. But before continuing the story, one last character must be introduced, one who was to become as important as Rado himself. Thanks to him, the 'Centre' began to take notice of Roessler. He was an Englishman called Alexander Foote.

Foote's life had been a chaotic one—he seemed fated to become a secret agent. He was an anxious, insecure man. He belonged to that category of human beings that is perpetually unsatisfied. They love money, but abhor work. They are possessed by a lust for power but paralysed by timidity. They rage constantly at their own failure, but do nothing to escape from it. The profession of espionage provides them with that escape, since it satisfies all their needs. They choose it as soon as the opportunity arises. Foote did just this, without a moment's hesitation or reflection.

He was born in 1905 into a comfortable middle-class family. He was given a good education, but was incapable of benefiting from it. Failure seemed to dog his footsteps from the beginning. In two years, he passed from being manager of some business or other to being in charge of a garage, chief salesman in a shop and, finally, unemployed. Little more was needed to thrust him into the arms of the Communist Party. The Spanish Civil War had just begun— there, at last, was a cause worth defending.

In December 1936, Alexander Foote found himself near

Madrid in the British battalion of the International Brigade. His intelligence, his meticulous sense of order and his great manual dexterity were soon noticed by the political commissar of his unit, Douglas Springhall. Springhall was to be his Pygmalion; it was he who made Foote into a spy.

In September 1938, Foote managed to flee from the dying Spanish Republic at the wheel of a Red Cross lorry, which he brought back with him to Britain. Through the influence of Springhall, Foote was shown the exceptional favour of being invited to attend the conference of the British Communist Party in Birmingham. Foote had nothing to do at the conference and was bored. In fact, this had been no more than an excuse to get him out of Spain. When Foote presented himself at the party headquarters in King Street in London, some days after the conference, a surprise was in store for him. Instead of being sent back to the front, he was offered a special job, for which he had been warmly recommended by Douglas Springhall. It meant working for the Soviet Union as a secret agent in Europe.

His political commissar had not misjudged him: Foote accepted without batting an eyelid. He then went to St John's Wood, the headquarters of the resident-director in London, where the initial formalities were quickly performed and he was given a parcel of instructions. He was to go to Geneva. On October 10, 1938, he was to be outside the General Post Office in the rue du Mont-Blanc, wearing a white scarf round his neck and holding a leather belt in his right hand. At noon, a woman would approach him and ask him the time. In a string bag on her arm, there would be a green parcel, and in her hand an orange. This woman would be his contact.

The woman was none other than 'Sonia', the experienced Ursula Schultz. She was somewhat surprised by the choice of the recruit. This completely inexperienced Englishman had a lot to learn. She gave him two thousand Swiss francs and sent him to Munich, advising him to learn German and behave like a tourist—and to keep his eyes and ears open. Three months later, on January 10, 1939, Foote met 'Sonia' again in front of the Post Office in Lausanne. This time 'Sonia' noticed that the Englishman had improved his German considerably, that he was not a spendthrift, since the money had been enough for his needs and, more important, that he was a good listener. He had discovered that when in Munich Hitler always lunched at the same restaurant, the Osteria Bavaria, near the Karlsplatz. Foote became excited and suggested that he should organise an attempt on Hitler's life—he had already studied the terrain. 'Sonia' cooled his ardour and told him to go on observing and learning. This time she sent him back to Munich with nine hundred dollars. He was not to come back before May or June—and she would get in touch with him. One of her agents in Germany would call and see him in April and give him more money.

Foote already knew this agent. He was one of his friends from the International Brigade, William Philips—who was now engaged in studying, for the Russians, the production of one of the factories of the I. G. Farben group, at Frankfurt. In August 1939, Ursula Schultz urgently called her two British spies to Vevey. The 'Centre' had warned her that the war was about to break out. And as there would be no new work for them for the time being they were to learn wireless-telegraphy. So Bill Philips and Foote took up residence in a modest boarding-house in Montreux. Every day, they went up to Caux and practised on Ursula's transmitter-receiver. By January 1940, Foote had become a very competent operator and was able to communicate with the 'Centre' on Ursula's behalf—which suited her perfectly well. She felt more and more bored by her job—and, in any case, she had suddenly fallen in love with William Philips.

Seven months later, in August 1940, the MGB ordered Alexander Foote to go to Geneva and there place himself temporarily at the disposal of Rado, long enough to teach Margareta Bolli and Edmond Hamel how to use the transmitter-receivers. Each of them had been supplied with the latest models. Bolli had hidden her set at her home in the rue Henri Mussard, in the Eaux-Vives district. Hamel had no difficulty in concealing his, for about five hundred yards away, near the Parc Alfred Bertrand, at 192 route de Florissant, he had a radio shop, with a repair workshop. Hamel had already studied radio-engineering in Paris, but strangely enough he proved the least gifted of the three as a Morse operator.

The 'Centre' decided that Foote should act as wireless-operator. Rado would communicate all urgent and important information to him—Hamel and Bolli would deal with more everyday information. Foote should not remain in Geneva, but go to Lausanne—thus reducing the chances of being rounded up by the Swiss authorities. His signal was to be NDA and his call-sign FRX. 'Sonia' and Philips resigned from the service and, in November 1940, they were given permission to settle in Britain. On December 20 they left for London, via Lisbon.

Meanwhile, Foote had found a flat, at 20 Chemin de Longeraie, on the top floor of a large building. The visitor had to pass through two heavy, well-locked doors to get into the flat itself, thus providing the occupant with a veritable flooding-chamber. Foote was delighted with this ideal strategic arrangement. If intruders forced their way into his retreat he would have ample time to sabotage his transmitter-receiver set and to destroy his files and codes.

Foote's first concern on moving in was to find a radio mechanic willing to set up an aerial right round his flat—an indispensable requirement if he was to correspond with Moscow effectively. To the electrician who carried out the installation, Foote passed himself off as an eccentric English millionaire who had been trapped in Switzerland by the outbreak of the war and wished to be able to hear the BBC broadcasts with perfect clarity.

The care Foote took over his 'cover' shows that in a very short time he had transformed himself from an amateur spy into an experienced agent. In fact, Foote's dramatic talents were such that he became accepted at face value by the colony of retired British army officers and civil servants living in Lausanne, at Ouchy. They seemed to see nothing unusual in the fact that a capricious bachelor showed an obvious disinclination to invite them to his home, or that the rhythm of his life should be peculiar to himself—he rose late, did little during the day and wrote, it seemed, well into the night.

This mask also confounded the aliens department of the Swiss police who came to make enquiries shortly after Foote moved in. He put on a masterly performance for the benefit of the two deferential police inspectors who called on him, offering them the best whisky and showing them bank statements that left no doubt as to his private means—'Sonia' had left him with the funds of the 'Centre' before leaving for England.

Of course, he said, he realised that he was really breaking the law concerning foreigners in the Confederation. He knew that he ought to reside in one of the hostels or camps that had been put at their disposal. But he hated crowds and wanted a place of his own. However, he had no desire to cause embarrassment to his hosts and was quite ready to do whatever they required of him. The tactics were successful. The inspectors agreed to allow him to occupy the flat, on condition that he paid six months' rent in advance and that he came every two weeks to the police station to sign the aliens' register.

Every two weeks Foote also went to Geneva—but this time on orders from the 'Centre'—to meet Alexander Rado in his offices at the Géo-Presse. The MGB had also fixed the times for the transmissions to be made: twice a week, on Wednesday and Saturday evenings, Foote would send out his messages.

So, from the first week of January 1941, Foote launched his appeals:

NDA FRX . . . NDA FRX . . . NDA FRX . . .

Moscow did not reply. Foote did not even know if he was being heard, but he persevered. Suddenly, on Wednesday, March 12, 1941, at 1.30 am, Foote received, very clearly, a reply: NDA OK QSR5 . . . NDA OK QSR5 . . .

A few seconds later there followed a series of five letters

and five figures, concealing the agreed code. The dexterity of the Moscow operator was so great that Foote was unable to keep up and asked him to begin again. The message was an important one. Following a series of reverses, most of the networks in Germany had been wiped out. The MGB could not therefore put much credence in the little information that continued to arrive from the survivors. It was vital for the Soviet Union that the Rado network begin operations.

On the night of March 15, 1941, Alexander Foote hardly had a moment's sleep. Rado had given him an enormous quantity of news for Moscow. There was information from 'Pakbo', 'Lili of the Vatican' and 'Isaac'. But these were all swamped by the extraordinary revelations of 'Lucy'—that is, Rudolf Roessler.

On February 20, 1941, said 'Lucy', the Germans had massed 650,000 men in Rumania, near the Ukraine border. On the night of February 28, other German divisions crossed the Danube and took up positions in Bulgaria, following a secret agreement made three weeks before between List, the special envoy of the OKW, and the High Command in Sofia. These troops were intended by Hitler to occupy Greece, in the event of the Allies deciding to open a front above Salonika, as in 1914, and thus upset 'Operation Barbarossa'. There followed a long report on Hitler's plans for the invasion of Russia.

On March 19, the 'Centre's' sharp reply came as a disappointment to Rado. How could this resident-director imagine that Moscow would accept information from someone of whom they knew no more than a code-name, and who, moreover, required as a condition of his co-operation complete secrecy concerning his sources? The information communicated by this 'Lucy' would be sensational—if true. They were so detailed that they could almost have come from the OKW itself! 'Lucy' should not be trusted. He was probably an agent-provocateur.

9

DURING THOSE FIRST FEW months of 1941, Rudolf Roessler must have been sorely tempted to give up completely. It may well be that the obstinacy and determination shown by this frail-looking man played no small part in making this resistance story so different from any other.

Through his ten friends in the headquarters of the Oberkommando of the Wehrmacht, this man was to know, before the rest of the world, the details of all Hitler's decisions, from 1939 to the end of April 1945. The chiefs of staff to whom Hitler delivered his orders seldom remained in contact with the Führer for long—being replaced in their jobs after a matter of months, sometimes even weeks. Rudolf Roessler was therefore the only man to have had continuous knowledge of the events that were to convulse the world. And he was well aware of the importance of every piece of information that passed through his hands. It was this knowledge, this sense of being at the centre of world events, that sustained him in those early days of disillusion and impotence, when first the Allies, then the Russians refused him credence.

Most men, as La Bruyère remarked, are more capable of a single great effort than of long perseverance in the pursuit of their aims. But Roessler was not like other men. He persevered—knowing that in the end he would overcome the Russians' mistrust. So, on March 27, 1941, despite the rebuff he had been given a week before, he contacted Christian Schneider. He had just received news of the greatest importance. Hitler had decided to delay 'Operation Barbarossa' for another four weeks. It had originally been planned for May 15, 1941. If the Russians deigned to listen this time they would have time to prepare themselves.

Roessler then went to the Villa Stutz to inform the Swiss, his initial employers, to explain the reasons for the delay. Twenty-four hours before, a popular uprising, supported by a majority of the army, had overthrown Prince Paul the regent of Yugoslavia, who had shown himself to be sympathetic to Nazi Germany. The young heir to the throne, Peter II, had been declared king. General Simovich immediately proposed a non-aggression pact with Germany. But the people had openly shown their hostility to the Führer by insulting his ambassador in Belgrade. Hitler was furious. He had been defied by a minor nation and decided to take wholesale reprisals. He immediately decreed his Directive No 25, addressed to the operational headquarters of the OKW.

"The military *coup d'état* in Yugoslavia has altered the political situation in the Balkans. Despite her professions of loyalty, Yugoslavia must be regarded from now on as an enemy of Germany and be brought to heel as soon as possible. I therefore intend to invade her as well as Greece and wipe out their armies. Operations will begin at dawn on April 6, 1941. As a result, 'Operation Barbarossa' will have to be delayed by four weeks."

Roessler insisted that the Allies should be warned in time of this new upheaval in that part of Europe. He was a good enough strategist to realise that the loss of these territories would constitute a serious blow to Britain. On the other hand, he was greatly relieved at the postponement of the invasion of Russia.

"This is a serious strategic error," he told the Bureau Ha, in his analysis of the situation. "This delay of a month will certainly prevent the Wehrmacht from achieving its objective. It will be stopped by the terrible Russian winter. This error should favour the free world. And all this to satisfy Nazi pride!"

From that day, Thursday, March 27, Roessler was in daily contact with his sources in Berlin. Each time, Roessler informed first Christian Schneider, alias 'Taylor', then the Swiss at Kastanienbaum. The Swiss never seemed to mind this order of precedence—for them what mattered was that they should be kept informed. In Rado's organisation, on the other hand, there was increasing embarrassment. What were they do do with 'Lucy's' information?

On Saturday, March 29, despite the orders from the 'Centre' not to take any notice of this dangerous source, Rado asked Foote to warn Moscow that evening that the mysterious 'Operation Barbarossa' had been postponed for four weeks. The MGB's answer on Wednesday, April 2, was hardly reassuring. It was a short, sharp condemnation. "Stop listening to this nonsense."

Alexander Rado did not insist further. Each of the reports transmitted by 'Taylor' got no further than his office. On April 25 a violent argument broke out between the head of the network and his 'cut-out', Schneider having guessed from his boss's lack of interest that his friend's messages were no longer leaving Geneva.

"We cannot go on dealing with your German friend while he persists in concealing the sources of his information."

"He will never reveal them."

"How do you know that this man isn't trying to use us?"

"You are making a serious mistake, comrade. It's madness, treason. The Nazis are about to invade the Soviet Union. And if they win the war, because Moscow didn't know all there was to know of their plans, then you will be partly responsible."

"I'm covered. The 'Centre' has given instructions that they wish to hear nothing more of your 'Lucy'."

"Send them the news all the same! It's your mission, your duty. I can't give you any convincing proof. But I can answer for him. He's as much an anti-Nazi as you or I."

"It's no use insisting. I'm not sending anything."

"Have you at least read the latest messages? The 17th German Armoured Division, which was in central Poland, is now encamped in the Chelm forests within gunshot range of Russian territory. What's it doing there? General Stülpnagel's 17th Army is advancing towards the Ukrainian border. What's it going to do there? Did you know that the Skoda works in Czechoslovakia has been ordered by Berlin to stop taking orders for arms from the Soviet Union? Why?"

"It's no use. I shan't send all this."

Schneider walked out and banged the door of the Géo-Presse offices. Next day, he took the train for Lucerne to meet Roessler at the Vita Nova Verlag. He briefly explained the attitude of the resident-director, trying rather clumsily to offer excuses for Moscow's decision. Roessler said that he understood. No one wanted to face up to the truth. But he would not give up.

"Unfortunately, my dear Schneider, events will prove that we were right to persevere. Moscow will listen to us then."

Throughout May 1941, the Russians heard no more of 'Lucy's' activities. But he had not been idle. Day after day he had communicated to Christian Schneider, then to the Swiss, the movements of the Wehrmacht towards the Soviet frontiers—the group of armies under General von Leeb in the north, with twenty-one infantry divisions and six armoured divisions; Field Marshal von Rundstedt's troops in the south, with seventeen infantry divisions, four mountain divisions, four divisions of mobile infantry and five armoured divisions; and a formidable armada under Field

Marshal von Bock in the centre, with thirty infantry and fifteen armoured divisions. Over a front of 1,600 kilometres, 3,000,000 men, 750,000 horses, 600,000 cars, 7,200 guns, 3,000 tanks and 1,800 planes were awaiting 'D' day, at 'H' hours.

Roessler had enumerated everything in detail. It was an extraordinary piece of work on his part. He had also described the state of mind of the troops concentrated at Tilsitt, Insterburg, Zichenau, Chelm, Bialystock, Przemysl and Iassy. Above all, he had placed particular emphasis on the invasion plans that this enormous war machine had been given to carry out. Von Leeb's mission was to cross the Memel, wipe out the Russian troops throughout the Baltic states and move on to Leningrad. His spear-head would be General Hoepner's armoured divisions. Von Bock's objective was first Smolensk, then Moscow—with two groups of armoured troops commanded by the best generals in the Wehrmacht, Guderian and Hoth. Von Rundstedt would make a break-through between the Pripet Marshes and the Carpathes, invade the Ukraine and, if possible, reach Kiev.

The strategy worked out by the Oberkommando of the Wehrmacht seemed perfectly clear. A great effort would be made in the centre, across a marshy region crossed by a great many rivers, where they would be least expected. The Russian front would be broken and the Russian armies encircled in a number of pockets. In the same movement all the great vital centres would be occupied.

Throughout that May and the first week of June 1941, Alexander Rado hardly slept in his fine flat at 113 rue de Lausanne in Geneva. He read and re-read the information from 'Lucy'. Perhaps the 'Centre' was wrong after all? Why not trust him? He couldn't get Christian Schneider's words out of his mind. "You will be partly responsible." The Kremlin had never had any difficulty in finding a scapegoat when things went wrong!

Curiously enough, Alexander Foote offered the same reasoning when the two men met some days later, on

Thursday, June 12, 1941. The night before, Schneider had been to see Rado. They had hardly been on speaking terms since the altercation of April 25. Schneider had simply placed a piece of paper on Rado's desk. Rado could hardly believe his eyes when he read the message written on it: "General attack on territories occupied by Russians dawn of Sunday, June 22: 3.15 a.m."

When Schneider had satisfied himself that Rado had taken in the message, he turned on his heels and went out without a word. All night Rado turned over the short message in his mind. On the morning of Thursday, June 12, he could bear it no longer. He telephoned Foote, which he had never done before. Sounding deeply moved, he asked the Englishman to come at once to Geneva. Having insisted that Rado should meet him at the Gare de Cornavin at noon, Foote cursed and hung up.

The two spies walked in silence down the rue du Mont-Blanc to the bridge that closes Lake Leman at the point where the Rhône continues on its way into France. They then turned left and stopped at a distance from the casino, in front of the landing-stages, which in peace-time were used by pleasure boats. There, on a bench overlooking the Lake, Rado handed Foote the message.

"What are you going to do?" Foote asked.

After a long silence, Rado murmured: "What can I do? You know how sceptical the 'Centre' was about 'Lucy's' information. This information may *not* be true?"

Foote made no secret of his annoyance:

"So you've brought me all the way here just to tell me that you haven't made up your mind yet! If I were you, I'd send the information all the same. It would then be up to the 'Centre' to accept responsibility. Who knows, you might later be accused of criminal negligence. And I wouldn't like to be in your shoes then."

The prospect of what lay ahead if this were the case suddenly forced Rado into making a decision. He gave Foote the message.

"Send it at the next normal transmitting time, the day

after tomorrow. Come back to my office with me and I'll give you a dossier I've got in my safe—all the information sent in by 'Lucy' for the past month. Ask the 'Centre' to give you three or four extra transmitting times—you'll need them to send that lot out. Never mind if they don't like it. At least we'll have done our duty."

So on June 14, then on 16, 17 and 18, 1941, Alexander Foote kept at his transmitter—and the only answer he got was, "Understood. Over." When he had finished burning all the papers and all his code jottings, Foote collapsed on his bed, exhausted. He slept for the next twenty-four hours. He would have liked to have kept a copy of all this exceptional information for his own later use, but the orders of the MGB were that everything must be destroyed.

This time, the Russians showed no suspicion of 'Lucy's' information. So many other sources simply confirmed the date of the invasion, that they would have been mad not to believe the rest, which was infinitely more important. In fact, the date, June 22, had been confirmed by Richard Sorge, the best Soviet agent in the Far East. Moreover, Cordell Hull and Sumner Wells, the American Secretary and Under-Secretary of State, had just warned Constantin Umansky, the Soviet ambassador in Washington, that they had received information from their legations in Europe of a planned invasion of Russia by the Germans. Finally, the date had also been confirmed by Churchill who had got wind of it through his espionage network in Germany.

The MGB was in a ferment of doubt. The arguments were gone over time and time again. Had Stalin perhaps been wrong to base everything on the non-aggression pact signed with Hitler? Was he not making a terrible mistake in not alerting the four and a half million soldiers of the Red Army at the frontier? The Army High Command had been wanting this for a long time. Moreover, there were other facts—apart from information that had come from espionage sources—that indicated that something was going on beyond the western frontier.

In the past two months, twenty-four German reconnaissance planes had flown well into Soviet territory. One of them had crashed. Top-quality cameras had been found in the wreckage, with film that left no doubt that their sole mission had been to photograph Soviet military installations. Moreover, for the past three months, German firms that should have fulfilled the terms of the economic contract signed on January 10, had stopped sending their goods to the USSR. The Russians, however, had proved their good faith by increasing their supplies of cereals, petroleum, ferrous and non-ferrous metals and rubber. Lastly, well-informed newspapers throughout the world, which were attentively studied every day in the Ministry of Security, made continual references to concentrations of German troops on the Russian frontiers. Yes, Stalin might well have been wrong.

Although Stalin had forbidden any defensive moves to be made along the frontiers, fearing that they might be interpreted by Hitler as acts of defiance, the MGB sent a discreet warning to the Red Army High Command..

But the results of the 'Centre's' belated meditations could no longer spare the Soviet Union. Hidden in the dense Polish fir forests, under the oaks, beeches and ashes of the Carpathes and amid the cane-apples and laurels of Bessarabia, 146 divisions, of which 102 would carry out the first assault, lay ready to attack.

The men were in peak condition and in high morale, and dreamt of succeeding where Napoleon had failed. In Berlin, Ribbentrop, the German Foreign Minister, was already composing the coded message that would be sent to his ambassador in Moscow, Count Karl Schulenburg—it was one of the Führer's most cynical declarations of war: "Information received in the past few days by the government of the Reich leaves no doubt as to the aggressive nature of Soviet troop movements. Moreover, information from a British source has confirmed the existence of negotiations conducted by the British ambassador, Sir Stafford Cripps, with a view to close military co-operation between Great Britain and the Soviet Union. The government of the

Reich declares that in violation of its solemn engagements the Soviet government has been guilty:

"*a*—of having continued and intensified its manoeuvres with a view to undermining Germany and the rest of Europe.

"*b*—of having assembled on the German frontier all its armed forces on a war footing.

"*c*—of making preparations, of an obvious kind, and in violation of the German-Russian non-aggression pact, to attack Germany.

"As a result, the Führer has ordered the armed forces of the Reich to meet such a threat with every means at their disposal."

Towards the end of the afternoon of June 21, 1941, an embarrassed von Schulenburg presented Molotov with this message in the latter's office in the Kremlin. Nine hours later, on a front of more than a thousand kilometres, a wave of fire swept across Russian territory. The war in the East had begun.

On June 23, 1941, Rudolf Roessler was to discover two of the 'Centre's' best qualities: a profound contempt for wounds inflicted on its *amour-propre* and a remarkable capacity to adapt itself to changing circumstances. For two and a half months, the Russians had stubbornly kept their hands over their ears, refusing to listen to 'Lucy's' shouts of alarm. Suddenly, overnight, their attitude was transformed: they offered the despised 'Lucy' the largest emoluments that had ever been paid to a secret agent and begged him to continue to work for them to the maximum of his capacities.

In fact, the night before, the very same day as the German attack on the Soviet Union, Alexander Foote tuned his transmitter-receiver on to the same wavelength as was usually used by the MGB. It was not his usual day for transmitting and he was afraid he would get no reply. But disturbed by the new turn taken by the Second World War, he felt a deep need to be in touch with Moscow.

Suddenly, Foote was startled by an increasingly sharp whistle in his head-phones. Someone was on the wavelength.

The whistle stopped and was followed by a series of two dashes and two dots: Z,Z,Z,Z. It was the 'Centre'. Foote recognised at once the 'signature' of his Moscow counterpart. A flood of letters and figures arrived as usual. Then silence. Foote made use of the break to translate the hermetic mass of signs:

"Calling all networks . . . Calling all networks. The fascist beasts have invaded the workers' fatherland. The moment has come to do all in our power to help the USSR in its struggle against Germany. Signed, the Director."

After a short interval, the 'Centre' continued its transmission:

"NDA . . . NDA . . . NDA . . . Special message."

NDA was Foote.

"NDA . . . The 'Centre' has decided that from now on dispatches will be divided into three categories. 'MSG' will designate routine communications, 'RDO' urgent messages and 'VYRDO' will preface messages of the greatest importance. From today all information communicated by 'Lucy' will be classified as 'VYRDO' and be sent on immediately. The 'Centre' will be available to receive communications twenty-four hours a day. NDA alone will transmit 'Lucy's' communications. 'Edwards' and 'Rosie' will be duly informed . . ."

'Edwards' and 'Rosie' were, of course, Hamel and Margareta Bolli, Rado's personal wireless-operators. Things must be getting very serious, Foote thought. Within a few seconds, he was left in no doubt. He was ordered by the MGB to contact 'Lucy' at once. All his information was anxiously awaited in Moscow. He was to be paid a regular salary of 7,000 *Swiss francs a month*, which would not include additional payments for exceptional information. In 1941, a monthly salary of 7,000 Swiss francs was something of a fortune.

10

MONEY DID NOTHING TO change Rudolf Roessler's habits. He continued to rise at 6.30 every morning, ate his frugal breakfast of coffee and toast, and at 7.30 left his home to catch the tram, which took him to the centre of Lucerne. At 8 he opened the Vita Nova book-shop in the Fluhmattstrasse. He devoted his mornings to his correspondence and to the day-to-day affairs of the publishing business. At noon he went home to lunch. His tastes in food were extremely simple, not to say ascetic. His clothes were few—and he used them until they were worn out: a dark, ready-made suit, a long, black overcoat for winter, an equally long mackintosh for other seasons, and a soft, felt hat that he wore pulled down to his ears.

Roessler did not smoke—he suffered from frequent and very tiring attacks of asthma. He appeared to have only one weakness: coffee. He drank coffee all day, at home, at the office and at the Villa Stutz at Kastanienbaum—and well into the night.

Roessler devoted his afternoons to his work for the

Swiss secret service, correlating and evaluating all the information they supplied him with for the use of Brigadier Masson. The head of the Swiss intelligence service always took Roessler's reports with him when he attended the meetings of the Swiss High Command organised for General Guisan. After dinner, Roessler became once more an active agent, engaged on the wireless-telegraphy that linked him to his friends in the Oberkommando of the Wehrmacht. He often worked until three o'clock in the morning, decoding and writing up the dispatches from *Werther* and *Olga*. In addition, Rudolf Roessler never ceased to perform his role as 'Lucy', for ever at the disposal of Christian Schneider, his 'cut-out', finding time to transmit news concerning the Soviet Union to the Russians and to carry out the instructions he received from them.

He gave up going to the theatre and cinema, fearing that he might miss a transmission. He never took time off, either for a holiday or even for a weekend. The Russians paid him well and he accepted their money. Christian Schneider had insisted that if he did not Moscow might begin to be suspicious again. But even if he had not been paid by the 'Centre' he would not have worked a jot less for them. He cared for nothing but the defeat of Nazism.

"Above all, tell 'Lucy' that he must not worry about the payments in the event of delays," the director of the 'Centre' declared on June 25, 1941.

Then, again, on June 30 of that year:

"Make it perfectly clear to 'Lucy' that in the event of irregularities in the payment of his salary he must be patient and in no way slacken his efforts at this important time in our struggle against Hitler. We will never fail to meet our obligations."

'Lucy' could not have cared less. For, contrary to the image the MGB had created of him, he was not in the least mercenary-minded. Alexander Rado, on the other hand, was always preoccupied with financial matters. Up to June 21, 1941, things had been relatively easy. The economic service of Vladimir Dekanozov, the Soviet ambassador in Berlin, had been instructed to provide a plentiful flow of money for the network. The only difficulty was in getting the money into Switzerland: Rado solved this problem by simply getting one of his agents to bring the money in secretly.

When the Berlin embassy was closed, Moscow ordered the resident-director of its last espionage network in Europe, to get its supply of funds from the Swiss Communist Party and these advances would be repaid later. Unfortunately, Léon Nicole's party was itself short of money and said that it would be unable to comply. Rado lost his temper and the 'Centre' became increasingly angry. At this point Foote thought up a simple scheme based on trust.

Some of his British acquaintances in Lausanne would put him in touch with one of the directors of the Lausanne branch of an important American company. For the benefit of this American, he would play up his role of eccentric and extravagant millionaire and ask help in getting money into Switzerland. He would say that he'd be willing to pay the black market rate of interest. All that was needed was for the MGB, through a person who could not be suspected of working for the Russians, to credit the bank account of this company in New York with the money required. The company would then credit its Lausanne branch with an equivalent sum in Swiss francs. The branch would then hand over the money to Foote after subtracting the agreed commission.

The 'Centre' agreed to the idea at once. Nothing could be easier than sending money to the United States. The director of the Lausanne branch also agreed, believing he was doing a good turn to a rich English gentleman. The company in New York did not object either, being quite unaware that involuntarily it was helping to finance a Soviet espionage network. Neither the directors of the company in New York, nor the American in Lausanne, seemed to express the least surprise at the size of the sums transferred in this way. None of these transactions took more than ten days to complete—which must have been a record for those troubled times.

It might be said that the MGB was the only part of the Soviet war machine to work effectively against Nazi Germany in the first months of the war. Elsewhere, on the fronts, the Russian soldiers, whose job the MGB should normally have made easier, collapsed under the German attack and the enormous advantage which the Russians possessed, of knowing the enemy's plans in advance, was at first of little use. The information had come too late and the Russians needed time to recover from the first unexpected blows, before they could benefit fully from their good fortune. This took three months—during which time the Germans began to suspect that some deadly parasite had got into their system and was sapping them of their strength.

In fact, on July 2, ten days after the beginning of the war in the East, 'Lucy' confirmed to the MGB that the German plan of attack had Moscow as its immediate objective. Most of the German effort would be flung into the central front by the tanks of Guderian and Hoth. The troop movements in the north and south would be little more than diversions. This was what the Oberkommando of the Wehrmacht had called 'Plan I'.

On July 27, 1941, 'Lucy' asked Rado to warn the 'Centre' at once that the OKW, sensing that the Russians were building up their resistance on the central front, had suddenly switched to 'Plan II'. This plan involved two main thrusts, from the north and south, in a pincer movement, thus giving some respite to the troops of Field Marshal von Bock.

These were obviously two quite vital pieces of information. If the Red Army was incapable of containing the German advance on all fronts, at least its commander-in-chief, Marshal Boris Mikhailovich Shaposhnikov, was able to communicate at once to the corps commanders at the front those parts of 'Lucy's' information that were relevant to them. As a result, there was an important change of tactics, accompanied by an avalanche of details concerning the units that the Soviet troops would find in front of them.

Nevertheless, on August 10, 1941, the fighting post

headquarters of the 16th Russian Army fell intact into the hands of General Hoth's panzer-grenadiers, east of Smolensk. The military security officers blew open the door of a rusty safe and were stupefied to find, among a mass of paperwork, exact copies in Russian of the OKW's two plans of campaign, as well as a copy of the sudden decision to adopt the second of the two.

A few days before this discovery, the German military security officers had found another packet of confidential papers, in an office abandoned by the general commanding the 1st Cossack Army, at Lomza. To their amazement, they realised that the Red Army knew of the weak spot in the organisation of the German Army. This Achilles' heel of the Wehrmacht in 1941, and which, despite successive improvements, was to remain a vulnerable point, was supplies. Rudolf Roessler, or 'Lucy' for Rado and the Russians, never ceased to interest himself in this problem throughout the war. The first information on the subject, which he gave to Christian Schneider for transmission to Moscow, was as early as June 27, 1941; it had taken Alexander Foote four hours to transmit.

"Throw everything into the attack," was invariably Hitler's orders when drawing up his plans of campaign—and the OKW complied. As a result, the Oberkommando of the Wehrmacht was no longer capable of making large-scale plans for retreat when things no longer went in their favour. The Wehrmacht appeared to have one universal tactic: concentrate all available troops in a single overwhelming break-through and annihilate the enemy in one blow.

The assault plans of the OKW were really very remarkable and could be studied with profit by military schools even today. The same cannot be said for their support organisation, which was far too unwieldy ever to be adapted to shock tactics. Hitler decreed that the German soldier was not to feel weighed down in his lightning attacks. No special supply service would be attached to the fighting units. Food, ammunition, fuel, spare parts, even medical supplies would be taken as close to the fighting line as possible and placed in clearings where the combatants would come and supply their needs.

These clearings were obviously enormous. For an infantry division of the Wehrmacht consumed 130 tons of general supplies a day; a panzer division, 300 tons; an army, 5,000 tons; and a group of armies, such as those under von Bock, von Leeb or von Rundstedt, 18,000 tons—18,000 tons a day, the equivalent of 36 train-loads! It was this fact that was inevitably to sap the Wehrmacht's strength.

One has only to imagine the long cohorts of vehicles from the fighting units coming back to the rear lines to get their food and supplies and the inextricable traffic jams around these monstrous depots. This is exactly what it was like on the Eastern front, against a background of dust, mud or snow, according to season. These vast compounds provided a magnificent objective for the enemy air force. When the OKW strategists were preparing the 'Operation Barbarossa', first on a 1/1,000,000th map of Russia, published in 1896, then later on other more modern maps on a 1/500,000th scale, they carefully planned the sites for these vast mobile depots in relation to the advance into Russia, as well as the routes to be followed by the troops to reach the depots. These were the weak spots communicated by Rudolf Roessler to Rado, and which the Russians had faithfully copied on to their own maps.

For the Germans, this dramatic discovery at Lomza meant only one thing: the enemy seemed to be remarkably well informed. Perhaps they even had spies within the Wehrmacht itself!

This impression soon became a certainty, following an event that took place on the battlefield. On August 10, 1941, Rudolf Roessler informed Alexander Rado—as well as the Bureau Ha at Kastanienbaum—that the Wehrmacht High Command had decided to adopt a modified version of 'Plan I': the group of armies in the centre, commanded by Field Marshal von Bock, would attack again, through Briansk, in the direction of Moscow. General Halder, the chief of staff, only proposed this modified plan to the Führer on August 18. The OKW services in the camp at Zossen, near Berlin, worked at top speed on the practical details of this plan. Among the technicians involved in this work were Roessler's ten accomplices. Thus Roessler got full details of the plan eight days before it had been presented to the Führer. Stalin was immediately informed and he and Marshal Shaposhnikov decided to make a lightning attack on the Wehrmacht. This was the first Russian attack since the beginning of the conflict. On August 12 they called in the best tank technician, Erememko.

"Guderian will attack Moscow in a week's time," Stalin told him. "He will go through Briansk. I want you to take over the command of the defence of this front. I shall even send you as reinforcements the 3rd and 21st Armies which are at present in the Ukraine. We're safe there for the moment. You have a heavy task to accomplish."

It was then that history—and the Führer, whose sudden decisions were always unpredictable and enigmatic—played a dramatic trick on the Russians. On August 18, as 'Lucy' had said, Halder took his plan to Hitler, who was then in his wartime headquarters, Wolfsschanze, at Rastenburg, in East Prussia, a damp, densely wooded area. The conference lasted five days. Hitler seemed in a particularly gloomy mood, as the generals, whom he terrorised and even insulted without protest, awaited a decision.

The war was dragging too much for his taste. Moscow could wait. He wanted the Ukraine and its rich grain-fields. Guderian, who wanted to take the Soviet capital, which he felt was within the grasp of his tanks, could not change Hitler's mind.

"Attack at once in the south!" Hitler ordered. "Link up with von Rundstedt's armies. Attack and get me Kiev!"

This was the crucial moment that upset the predictions of Roessler's ten friends and confounded Stalin, who continued to prepare for the Briansk-Moscow operation and had transferred his defences from the Ukraine for that purpose. Roessler's friends knew nothing of the Führer's latest *volte-face*—and they were to learn nothing more for the next few days. This was because the OKW had had no hand in drawing up the latest plans for Guderian's break-through. Guderian had been left to exercise his own initiative as the occasion arose.

From August 20 to 25, 1941, Guderian's troops moved southwards exactly parallel to the lines held by Eremenko. A few stiff battles took place on the way when the two armies came into contact. But these were merely the work of Guderian's defensive flank. Eremenko was confused. Did Guderian intend to make a détour to the south and attack Briansk from the side? Guderian, too, was confused. Why did Eremenko not attack him from the side and try to break up his columns? What was he going to be met with in the Ukraine? Red Army units weakened by the departure of those armies mobilised by Stalin to defend Briansk, a scarcely defended route, then the advance guard of von Rundstedt's armies from the south. At the heart of this magnificent encirclement was Kiev, defended by troops under the famous, old Marshal Semyon Mikhailovich Budienny, a legendary figure of the Revolution. The Russians fought well, but Kiev capitulated. At one blow, the Wehrmacht wiped out half a dozen Soviet armies, took 660,000 prisoners and destroyed more than 1,000 tanks and 5,000 guns. For Stalin, it was a major disaster. For Hitler, it was a good sign; he now wanted Moscow.

With hardly time for a breathing space, Guderian now moved northwards. A month and a half after the original rendezvous with Eremenko, he arrived at Briansk. Guderian took the Soviet armies from behind and forced open their lines. Like Kiev, Briansk fell, then Viazma. The Wehrmacht now moved straight on to the Soviet capital. They were to get no farther than the city's outer suburbs, where they halted, exhausted and already handicapped by the approach of winter, for which they had made no preparations. The Germans did not yet know that this was to lose them the war.

However, their confidence was somewhat shaken by

what their Military Security service had discovered in the middle of October, among the ruins of Briansk—once more, documents, which explained Eremenko's inertia as Guderian's troops had moved almost under his nose. The Russian general had been expecting attack on positions that he knew to be impregnable if attacked head-on. These documents were a copy of 'Plan I', as revised by Halder and presented to Hitler on August 18 at Rastenburg!

Military Security then decided to hand over the results of these extraordinary discoveries to the Abwehr, the Wehrmacht's official organisation for espionage and counter-espionage. But as its head, Admiral Canaris, was already suspected of being not altogether faithful to the cause of the Führer, the Sicherheitsdienst, the security service of the Nazi Party, then directed by Reinhard Heydrich, was also informed.

The whole affair was at once regarded as being of vital importance by the most elegant of the Führer's disciples. Like Hitler, Heydrich had always detested the German officer corps. He had not forgotten that he had been discharged from the navy, in which he had hoped to make a career, for gambling debts and dishonourable actions. He was at once convinced that among that band of suspects, in whose charge the salvation of Germany rested, there was a traitor, or perhaps several, who were acting as Soviet informers. The exceptional nature of the discoveries made by Military Security on the Eastern Front proved that the leak must be among the officer corps. He must discover who they were at once.

Heydrich would have liked to have taken over the job himself, but he hadn't the time. He was one of the best horsemen and one of the finest fencers in Germany. Moreover, he was the lover of Himmler's wife and also of the wife of Koch, the Gauleiter of East Prussia. In any case, he was too preoccupied with intrigues within the party. So he decided to entrust the inquiry to his brilliant assistant, the young SS-Brigadeführer, Walter Schellenberg.

At Maybach camp at Zossen, only a few kilometres away

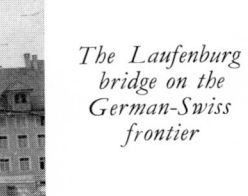

*The Laufenburg
bridge on the
German-Swiss
frontier*

Gastof Laufen

The Bahnhof Hotel at Waldshut

The embankment of the Rhine at Waldshut. The scene of one of the privat talks between Masson and Schellenberg

Wolfsberg, at Ermatingen, where Schellenberg spent his week-end visits to Switzerland

The hotel where the meeting between General Guisan and Schellenberg took place

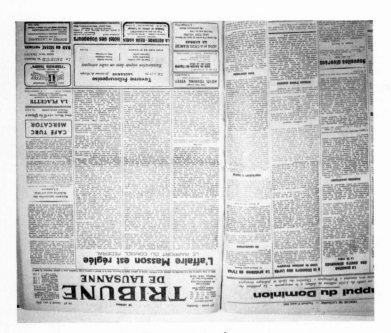

The 'end' of the 'Masson affair'

The beginning of the 'Masson affair'

from the headquarters of the Sicherheitsdienst, Rudolf Roessler's companions had no notion that the most formidable espionage organisation in the Reich was about to begin its attempts to localise the leak. They had no reason to fear. Did they not take every possible precaution? As soon as a piece of information of sufficient importance reached them, they coded it and awaited a suitable time at night, when the traffic was at its most intense, to transmit it. No listening station could distinguish this single transmission among the thousands of coded radio-telegrams being emitted into the atmosphere. And their messages could only be decoded in Lucerne.

Roessler had not realised that Stalin's sudden blind trust in 'Lucy' had caused a strategic catastrophe, the loss of Kiev. The 'Centre' made no reproaches. The affair would simply find its way to the profits and losses account. The Germans would pay for it later—with interest. The only urgent requests for information to come from Moscow concerned the German units on the Eastern front. How many men? How are they armed? What are their destinations? Roessler transmitted these requests to Berlin and the replies came back, usually within forty-eight hours.

At the beginning of autumn 1941, he was even able to pass on to the Russians two surprising items of scientific information. The Germans were putting the final touches to a new weapon, which had been called the 'V-1'. They had also begun the construction of a ten-ton rocket. This was one of the last messages to be transmitted by Alexander Foote before an incident took place that was to cause considerable concern to Roessler and to his friends in the OKW.

On October 19, 1941, a Sunday night, the operator at the 'Centre' in Moscow was transmitting a dispatch that had lasted about half an hour, involving requests for details on the activities of the Wehrmacht, when suddenly the Morse stopped dead. Foote made two or three calls, but there was no reply. The next day he tried again and again the day after that, but he was met by silence. He warned Rado, and

Schneider telephoned Roessler, but no one knew what was happening.

For the next six weeks, Roessler communicated his information only to his Swiss employers in the Bureau Ha. In Berlin, his friends became irate. It wasn't the Swiss who were fighting the Nazis! Some other means of communicating with the Russians had to be found.

Every night Foote tuned in his transmitter-receiver to the 'Centre's' wavelength in the hope that something would come through. Suddenly, on Monday, December 1, 1941, the 'Centre' resumed its transmissions. To Foote's great surprise, the Soviet operator continued to transmit the same message he had been communicating when the interruption occurred a month and a half earlier—as if those weeks of anxiety had never been! At the end of the dispatch, Foote asked his unknown colleague the reason for so prolonged a silence.

It was quite simple. Following a German attack on Moscow, the authorities had feared that the Soviet capital might be taken, or subjected to a long siege, and had decided to evacuate all the administrative services to Kuibyshev, the old city of Samara, now a port on the Volga. Every department of the bureaucratic machine had been warned in time, except the transmitting service of the 'Centre'. On October 19 they had had to move in the middle of a storm.

11

"CONTRARY TO THE PORTRAIT
of himself that Schellenberg presented to the British after
the fall of the Third Reich, that of a cultured man of
western, not to say Latin, tastes—and which many believed
to be true—I was never able to see in him anything other
than a faithful copy, a perfect reflection of Reinhard Heydrich. Even to the bearing of the head, the smile, the
presence—and the passion for horse-riding. Unfortunately,
he also had the same cold cruelty, the same profound
amorality, and the same aristocratic art of concealing his
vices! Heydrich was his intellectual master."

This astonishing portrait is provided by Hans Bernd
Gisevius, war-time German Vice-Consul in Switzerland,
and one of the organisers of the attempt on Hitler's life on
July 20, 1944. It explains the extraordinary similarity between
the actions of the two men. In the capture of the two British
agents at Venlo in Holland, on November 9, 1939, in the
manufacture of false pound-notes at Oranienburg and the
manipulation of the spy, Cicero—all operations conceived
by Schellenberg—there was the unmistakable imprint of

Heydrich. The two men complemented each other perfectly. The one had only to throw out a vague idea for the other to carry it out beyond all the hopes of its originator.

Thus, when one evening Heydrich happened to say that the Sicherheitsdienst ought to set up an establishment in which foreign visitors could come and amuse themselves in agreeable company, and where involuntarily they would give away valuable information, in a very relaxing atmosphere, Schellenberg began the next day to plan the famous 'Kitty Salon'. The prettiest German prostitutes, and ladies of the highest social standing came to perform their military service. Many a diplomat lost his self-control in this paradise filled with invisible microphones, tape-recorders and cameras. Following indiscreet revelations made in this *de luxe* brothel, situated in the heart of the fashionable quarter of Berlin of the period, Count Galeazzo Ciano, Mussolini's son-in-law, even lost his life.

It was also why, as soon as Reinhard Heydrich gave him the job of unmasking the traitors who were passing information to the Russians, that Schellenberg conceived a scheme that was entirely typical of its instigator.

Towards the end of October 1941 the SS-Brigadeführer drew up his plan of action. He would not attempt to go through the whole of the officer corps with a toothcomb to find the traitors—at least, not at once. There were no fewer than 3,000 generals and 320,000 other officers in the Wehrmacht! He decided he would concentrate his attention on the weak spot of most espionage organisations, the one which sooner or later gave most subversive networks away: wireless communications.

In fact, a particular affair that the Sicherheitsdienst had been studying persuaded Schellenberg to begin there. A network that had been working for the Russians, *Die Rote Kapelle*, and which had managed to distribute a large number of agents throughout Western Europe, had at last been caught. The SD had first intercepted, then decoded the messages of this network. Since then, most of the operators had been arrested, as they were transmitting their wireless-telegrams, by radiogoniometry. It was a simple matter to make these operators denounce their accomplices. One after another, the agents of *Die Rote Kapelle*, which had certainly paid little attention to secrecy measures, fell into the nets of the Sicherheitsdienst like ripe fruit.

It was in this fashion that Colonel Ozaki, the head of Japanese counter espionage, captured the famous Richard Sorge. Radiogoniometry was as disastrous an invention for secret agents as wireless-telegraphy had been for the countries on whom they were spying. A 'gonio' set is a simple receiver in which a mobile frame, pivoting on an axis, replaces the usual aerial. Experience and calculation had shown that the reception of a broadcast was always strongest when the frame was directed straight at the transmitting station. The position of the frame, therefore, indicated the geographical line on which lay the station the authorities were trying to track down. They only had to follow this line in order to catch the operators.

A 'gonio' set could also be used in another way, by orienting it so that the reception became minimal or disappeared altogether. The perpendicular to the frame then gave the required direction. Tripled and operated from three different points, the gonios were able to indicate precisely the position of an illegal transmitter. It was never long before the operators were seized.

One major reason urged Schellenberg to take an interest in the problem of broadcasts in order to find the traitors. Only a broadcasting station could be used to pass information to the Russians, but it was difficult to imagine a messenger service crossing the Wehrmacht's lines, bearing documents for the Russians—an unthinkable idea.

On Wednesday, November 5, 1941, the SS-Brigadeführer was near Dresden. The SD had just installed there an important new listening station. The best qualified decoders in Germany were engaged on work of capital importance. Not a decimetre of wavelength escaped their attention twenty-four hours a day. But in that incredibly enigmatic atmosphere it was often impossible to distinguish among the mass of dots and dashes those of the enemy. Even when an enemy message had been located it still did not yield up its secrets. It had to be worked on, often in vain. A 'B' never represented a 'B', either for the Führer's headquarters, for the transmissions of the OKW or for the enemy. Similarly, a '2' had no meaning in itself for this world of darkness. Sometimes, when the 'keys' to a code did not prove too difficult to break, as was the case of *Die Rote Kapelle*, for example, the experts in Dresden rejoiced. But their work was seldom as easy as that.

"Persevere!" Schellenberg told them. "One day you will find a series of suspicious signals in the atmosphere."

Chance seemed to smile on the SS-Brigadeführer. For three weeks he telephoned Dresden, anxiously hoping for news, and on November 28 the listening station informed him that on several successive nights they had made out a very brief message, repeated several times on 43 metres. On each occasion it had begun at exactly the same time, 1 a.m. The message was always the same: "NDA. FRX. . . NDA. FRX. . . NDA. FRX. . ."

"What do you think it is?" Schellenberg asked.

"Difficult to say. The brevity and the repetition of the signal would lead one to suppose that it was a call-signal."

"Where's it coming from?"

"It never lasts long enough for us to find out. We've no sooner got the gonio into position than the transmission stops."

"Keep trying!"

Paradoxically, it was this characteristic of patience that linked Schellenberg and Roessler; it is a quality shared by all the best secret agents. The most obstinate always win in this game of poker. The signal was, of course, that of Alexander Foote vainly calling the 'Centre' during the break in contact in December 1941. That Dresden had heard it was not, in itself, as serious as it might at first seem, for, following a principle that was practised by all clandestine operators, neither Rado's network, nor their opposite numbers in Moscow, ever used the same wavelengths for both their messages and their call-signals. Moreover, they used an additional camouflage. Foote called on 43 metres, then tuned on to 39 metres, as previously agreed with the 'Centre'. As soon as the 'Centre' had replied on 39 metres, Foote did not use 43 metres again. He would then communicate on the same wavelength as his Moscow colleague. These wavelengths were frequently changed to avoid establishing a pattern that could be picked up by a listening station.

Such a ruse could not hope to confuse for long specialists armed with the latest equipment. Dresden was well aware of the trick. They enlarged the area under observation, using several receivers simultaneously tuned-in to a range of neighbouring wavelengths. In order to limit the field in this atmospheric cacophany, they eliminated all the transmissions whose sources they knew, even if they did not know the wavelengths being used. These included, of course, the Oberkommando of the Wehrmacht and Hitler's own headquarters. Meticulously, they noted down thousands of fragments of enigmatic messages, cataloguing the incomprehensible, hoping that one day their rigorous classification of similar repetitions of letters and figures would provide a gleam of light that would put them on the track.

Meanwhile, events of the greatest importance were taking place in the world as 1941 came to an end. The German Army had just suffered its first setbacks in the East. Under pressure from General Zhukov, at the head of one hundred fresh divisions, the Wehrmacht was retreating before Moscow. Field Marshal von Kluge replaced von Bock as commander of the group of armies at the centre which had been unable to contain the T34s of Maslennikov and Koniev's divisions. Von Rundstedt had lost Rostov and had been deprived of his command. A series of dismissals had shaken the Wehrmacht High Command. Hitler had sacked Guderian and Hoepner on Christmas Day and taken over the supreme command of the German armed forces himself.

Even greater events had taken place. The United States had entered the war. Japan had transformed the war into a truly world conflict by making a lightning attack on Pearl

Harbour, on December 7, 1941. Britain had stoically sur-
vived its blitz. Reunion and Djibuti had joined Free France.
The suburbs of Zürich and Basle had been bombed by the
British in error.

The renewal of the radio link between Alexander Foote
and the 'Centre', now at Kuibyshev, had calmed Roessler's
fears. It was becoming urgent for his friends in the OKW,
who were becoming impatient. The news coming to Berlin
from the East showed, in fact, that if the Russians exploited
the Wehrmacht's first defeat to the full, Nazism might soon
be defeated. Never more than at this moment did the tiny
group of resisters have to struggle with their consciences.
Every dispatch communicated by them to the Russians
helped the Red Army to plunge into the living flesh of the
enemy—German flesh.

For the Soviet troops had at last recovered their nerve—
on all fronts, from the north to the south. In Crimea,
General Pervushin's troops were attacking those of Count
von Sponeck, Colonel von Choltitz and General Himmer.
On the Don, Timoshenko, Lopatin and Kharitonov had
recaptured Rostov and the 'Red Ruhr' that had fallen into
the hands of von Rundstedt. On the ice-bound region
before Moscow, the group of armies from the central front
were being harassed mercilessly by Zhukov, Kusnezov,
Belov and Dovator. At Staraya Russa, on the banks of
Lake Ilmen in the north, the soldiers of Morosov and
Eremenko were taking their revenge for the terrible
reverses they had previously suffered. A fantastic thrust west-
wards was beginning along a width of 1,000 kilometres,
as the Soviet tanks moved in after the retreating Germans.

Information from 'Lucy' had shown Stalin that the
Germans were in serious difficulties. They were still fighting
in their threadbare summer uniforms in a temperature of
−40° C. Snow got into their boots, turned into ice and
froze their feet—which then had to be amputated. The
Russians swept down on the retreating Germans—white
waves of men against a white background. Russians are
admirably suited to this kind of warfare. Wearing white

coats and white fur hats, the Siberian troops were ski-borne. Rifles, tanks and guns were painted white. The infantry wore boots that were always two sizes too big, which meant that their feet could be wrapped in rags—the famous red socks—and could swell in comfort. The cold, joining forces with the attacking spirit of the Russian soldier, delivered a blow to the Wehrmacht from which it never fully recovered.

The first complete figures for the German troops in Russia compiled by General Halder in that winter of 1941, were alarming. A retreat of 100 to 300 kilometres; 202,500 killed, 725,000 wounded, 46,500 missing, 112,500 frozen to death—a total loss of 1,100,000 men, a third of all the troops engaged at the beginning of the campaign. The Wehrmacht tried in vain to improve its transportation of supplies by organising a shuttle-service between the great supply depots and the front. It launched raids deep into Soviet-held territory. It motorised its troops as far as possible. But it had been irreparably weakened. It was to be finally eaten up by the steppes.

At the same time as General Halder, Rudolf Roessler was drawing up his own account. The early work of *Werther* and *Olga* had not borne much fruit. The western Allies had refused to listen to the mass of information that had been offered to them with such generosity. But the effects of their intervention in the East had been overwhelming. If the West had listened, Hitler could undoubtedly have been beaten in 1940.

The incredulity shown first by Copenhagen and Oslo, then by The Hague and Brussels and, finally, by London and Paris, shows quite simply that at the beginning of this monstrous war, the state of mind of the military high commands of the western democracies had not really evolved since 1918. For them, spies were still somewhat shady characters, unworthy of trust, even when they offered their information without expectation of reward!

In their wilful blindness these men had refused to see the signs of the coming Nazi cataclysm. As a result, millions of innocent people fell victim to their indifference. Oddly enough, even Stalin—who was much more aware of the value of a secret service than the western leaders—followed their example until the war actually reached his frontiers. But the first months of the campaign showed that the Russians were quick to recover from their initial suspicion. In the conduct of their operations, they were to value the information service at its true worth. Roessler was encouraged by their attitude and continued to work for them to his utmost.

The German émigré had another reason for his decision. The Swiss, at least those with whom he dealt—the Bureau Ha, Brigadier Roger Masson and, ultimately, General Guissan himself, the leading anti-Germans in the Confederation—allowed him to continue this collaboration with Moscow and thus acted as silent accomplices. With the entry into the war of the United States, these men felt considerably surer of their ground. Their decision, at the beginning of the war, to give tacit support to the Allies had been vindicated. By the winter of 1941-42, it was obvious that Germany, which had become a prisoner to Hitler, was unable to extricate itself from the situation in which the Führer had plunged it.

Information that had reached them through Rudolf Roessler showed the Swiss how badly things were going within the Reich: the grave defeats on the Russian front and the series of disgraces that had struck at the entire leadership of the OKW had revived the hopes of the many conspirators who flourished within the Wehrmacht High Command. Hitler, in fact, had dismissed thirty-five generals between December 1941 and January 1942—without counting Field Marshals von Brauchitsch, von Rundstedt, von Bock, von Leeb and Field Marshal von Reichenau, who had died of a blood-clot, and General Udet, of the Luftwaffe, who had committed suicide in November. With the return of these embittered soldiers to Berlin, the wind of revolt blew up once more.

The abortive attempt on Hitler's life on July 20, 1944, has been given a great deal of attention. In fact, it was merely the culmination of a line of earlier plots—all hatched by the same men, since 1938. Those who in 1944 were shot, or hung on butcher's hooks in Ploetzensee prison, or strangled with piano cord at Flossenburg, or driven to suicide, had previously tried no fewer than fifteen times to eliminate the Führer—according to the ups and downs in their careers.

In fact, it was a permanent, but really quite unserious conspiracy. It was doomed to failure because it included too many people. The whole army knew who they were. The Gestapo knew. Hitler himself knew. For when, after the failure of the attempt of July 20, he finally lost his temper and decided to strike back, 7,000 people were arrested, 5,000 of whom were summarily executed. In the corridors of the OKW the association of conspirators was irreverently known as 'The Barometer of Glory'. It went down only when the affairs of the Wehrmacht chiefs were going badly. Similarly, a stroke of good luck in the field, followed by a few judicious promotions by Hitler were enough to send the barometer soaring.

Rudolf Roessler's ten friends—but this was something the German émigré concealed from Masson and the Bureau Ha—kept well away from this vast, shifting mass of plotters, in order to do the better their own more destructive work. In fact, without knowing, these plotters were helping Roessler's friends, for whom they provided a convenient distraction. This explains why the ten men were so invulnerable within the Oberkommando.

Alarmed by the evident leaks that were taking place within this permanent nest of intrigue, the Sicherheitsdienst and the Gestapo made innumerable inquiries into its organisation, discovering without fail the currently suspect elements—but they never for a moment suspected the 'technicians' who were well known for their lack of interest in 'The Barometer'. Thus *Werther* and *Olga* passed through the nets which had been laid to catch them. Walter Schellenberg alone got close to them, and if history had granted Nazism a few more months of survival, he might well have caught them.

12

APRIL 1942—THE MUD SEASON
on the Eastern Front, a time of respite for the troops from
the Crimea to the Baltic. But the respite was not to be for
long. On each side of the front columns of new men and
materials were arriving from the rear lines to reinforce the
combatants. In Lucerne, Geneva and Lausanne, Roessler,
Rado and Foote were working at full stretch.

Thus on April 14 'Lucy' transmitted to the 'Centre', now
back in Moscow after the crisis of October 1941, the latest
decisions taken by the Führer in his headquarters at Rastenburg—a Hitler who was already going grey, suffered from
inexplicable fits of giddiness, and who seemed to be suffering
from a veritable phobia about cold and snow. Hitler had
obviously aged very quickly in the past few months, but his
lust for conquest was as strong as ever. He felt he had
nothing more to fear from the rancour of his generals,
since he was to provide them with work and with the
ultimate illusion of winning the war.

Rommel and his Afrika Korps had won a great victory.
His 'desert foxes' had recaptured Derna and Benghazi in

Cyrenaica and were preparing to take Tobruk and enter Egypt. The Führer hoped for even better things in Russia— nothing less than a complete, decisive victory. Or, at least, that is what he declared in his 'Directive No. 41' to the Wehrmacht. These ten pages of instructions were typed and sent off to the OKW—orders to be carried out. The December crisis having deprived him permanently of all confidence in his High Command he left his generals as little room for initiative as possible. He wanted to know everything and direct everything. All orders were to go out from Rastenburg, then from Berlin—a marvellous piece of fortune for *Werther* and *Olga*.

'Directive No. 41' was the plan of attack on the Don and the Caucasus. There were to be two simultaneous assaults: the first, in a pincer movement, on the Russian forces concentrated between the Donetz and the Don— which must be destroyed; the second, in a direct thrust, towards the Caucasian oil-fields. No sooner had the information reached the 'Centre', thanks to 'Lucy', than Stalin began to get restless—he wanted details, more details. Roessler transmitted the request to Berlin. On April 18 the reply came back.

Setting out from Kursk, Orel and Kharkov, half the group of armies in the south, under Field Marshal von Bock, would reach the Don, then follow its course to the great loop just before Stalingrad. The second half would attack from Stalino and the port of Taganrog, attempt to recapture Rostov, then link up with the first side of the pincer move- ment beyond the meeting at the Donetz. Finally, an army corps under Field Marshal List would have as its objectives the Caucasian hills and the Baku oil-fields. The dates of the opening of the offensive, then of the great attack itself were to be fixed later.

Completing his information, Roessler added that the long front line would then be defended by non-German troops. There would be fifty-two foreign divisions: twenty-seven Rumanian, thirteen Hungarian, nine Italian, two Czecho- slovak and one Spanish. Field Marshal Keitel had been sent to the Balkans to raise troops for the 'crusade' against Bolshevism. Hitler himself had obtained the Italians and Spaniards. The gaps made during the terrible winter months had to be filled. Because the Rumanians and Hungarians hated each other and were more likely to fight each other than the Russians, they would be separated by the nine Italian divisions and the one Spanish division. The German High Command, 'Lucy' added, were not depending too much on these reinforcements, being very doubtful of their military value.

The reservations of the German field marshals and generals were to prove only too well founded. These 'Legions' finally broke, and bore most of the responsibility for the Axis defeat. But in April 1942 neither the Germans nor the Russians knew this. No more than Foote knew that the listening-station of the Sicherheitsdienst, near Dresden, was rapidly tracking down the location of his transmitter.

In fact, in mid-April, Walter Schellenberg received a long report from his technicians. They had succeeded in recording a long series of mysterious dispatches—all coming from the same hand. They were now able to recognise his 'touch'. They were still trying to decode these dispatches. They felt that the use of series of five mixed letters and figures suggested the usual Soviet code systems, but it was too early as yet to make a positive decision on the matter.

They said they were using all the 'tracking' techniques at their disposal, but they needed time. However, they had already discovered an important fact. The transmitter that sent out these messages almost every night, always at the same time, was situated on a very definite geographical line, passing near Madrid, Saragossa, Toulouse, Lyon, Geneva and Nuremberg. The strength of the broadcast led them to suppose that the transmitter was not more than 1,000 kilometres away—which would exclude Spain.

They had undertaken systematic searches over the whole of the German territory crossed by this line, entrusting the southern part to the listening-post of Captain Frentznik, at Sigmaringen. The operator using this clandestine post frequently changed wavelengths, moving between 20 and 50 metres, but they had been able to draw up a table of his favourite frequencies.

Events accelerated during the next two months. In North Africa, Rommel launched his great attack on Tobruk. In the East, von Bock was preparing to launch his offensive. 'D' day had been fixed for May 18. But 'Lucy' informed the Russians in time, and they had known the date since May 5. At dawn on May 12, six days before the scheduled German attack, Timoshenko began to cut the ground from under the feet of the Wehrmacht.

The Russians had decided to split off the mass of the group of armies in the south in a pincer movement from the north with twenty-two divisions, six of them being armoured, and from the south, with sixty divisions, including fourteen armoured divisions. He aimed to get to Kharkov. Opposite him was the German 6th Army under von Paulus which was to sustain the brunt of his attack, and which was later to be destroyed at Stalingrad. In four days, everything seemed to be over. Completely cut off, von Paulus was unable to prevent Timoshenko from getting within twenty kilometres of Kharkov. A last effort and the Russian marshal would seize the town the Wehrmacht had organised as a depot to supply its troops during the planned offensive.

Timoshenko knew, thanks to 'Lucy', that at Kharkov he would find huge compounds of food and ammunition—both of which he needed urgently. His furious breakthrough had used up most of his reserves. His lines of communication had been stretched beyond a reasonable limit.

The red storm had no sooner broken than von Bock launched the Kleist group of armies, on May 18, after Timoshenko's rear lines. Three days later, in a sensational change of fortune, the Soviet attacking force was broken. Half their troops had been encircled and wiped out. The other half were in flight. There were 200,000 prisoners, and 2,000 guns and 1,000 tanks had been captured or destroyed.

In the south, too, things were going badly for the

Russians. Sebastopol was about to fall. Manstein and List were to find the roads to Stalingrad and the Caucasus wide open before them. Hitler was triumphant. He had not been able to enter Moscow, but he now had an even grander plan. He imagined Rommel occupying Egypt, then moving further east as far as the Persian Gulf. Rommel and List would link up to give him, at last, the Russian oil-fields, as well as those of the Arab world. He would then hold the fate of the whole world in his hands. Without oil who would be able to resist him?

In Berlin, Rudolf Roessler's friends were almost on the point of despair. The rejoicing that reigned in the German capital, and even within the OKW, because the gods of war had smiled once more on the Nazis, dismayed them. Everything seemed lost. What more could they do? They had taken maximum risks and sent maximum information to Roessler for the use of the Russians—plans of attack, details of the composition of the armies, of equipment and of supplies—always well ahead. But it had not been enough. They would have been even more despondent had they known of Schellenberg's jubilation.

Schellenberg was rejoicing because the only obstacle to his unbounded ambition had disappeared! Heydrich was dead. Jan Kubis and Josef Gabcik, two non-commissioned officers of the Free Czech Army, parachuted into Czechoslovakia by the RAF, had thrown a bomb under Reinhard Heydrich's Mercedes in Prague on May 27, 1942. He died, from infections in the wounds he had received, on June 4. But the Sicherheitsdienst was not headless for long. Two days later, before the body of Heydrich, exhibited with great pomp in the palace of the Wilhelmstrasse in Berlin, Heinrich Himmler—the head of the SS—summoned the party departmental chiefs. He said:

"I place Schellenberg at the head of the Sicherheitsdienst. The man lying here regarded him as worthy of the post and trained him for it. I, too, consider him to be capable of assuming the tasks that await him. Above all, he is incorruptible. His youth, and the fact that he is not a long-standing member of the National Socialist Party, should not prevent you too from adopting him.

"He is the youngest among us and for that reason has a right to my special support. I say this clearly, and in his presence, because it was the desire of your murdered chief that nothing should stand in the way of this nomination. And I consider Schellenberg to be too intelligent to allow himself to become intoxicated by what I have just said. On the contrary, I hope it will encourage him to carry out all the more carefully and attentively the tasks that will be assigned to him."

The second reason for Schellenberg's high spirits concerned the inquiry that had been entrusted to him by his late chief. He had made extraordinary progress. Before long, he might even be able to present Himmler with a valuable token of his thanks.

The listening-station at Sigmaringen had confirmed the researchs of the Dresden station. The general direction in which the clandestine transmitter was situated was definitely the Madrid-Nuremberg line. They did not yet know, however, to what point these regular dispatches were being directed. With the help of a powerful mobile station based in Strasbourg, a more precise triangulation had indicated that the transmitter was in Switzerland. It was as yet impossible to say whether it was in Geneva or Lausanne, but in any case it was somewhere on the shore of Lake Leman. This was a discovery of some importance for Schellenberg. The one that followed a week later, on June 18, 1942, was an even greater one.

Before the Second World War, Soviet espionage had begun to base the coding systems to be used by their secret agents for their transmissions on sentences taken from books. The Germans knew this. Their unmasking of *Die Rote Kapelle*, for example, had confirmed this. Moreover, their own information services were now using the same excellent method. It was natural, therefore, for the decoding division of the Sicherheitsdienst to direct its researches on these lines when it began work on the piles of dispatches recorded in Dresden since the beginning of 1941. After three months' extensive work the mathematical analysis section had succeeded in isolating a single obscure word among the mass of hieroglyphics: *Everhard*. A great many specialists in different fields had been set to work on the mysterious word, in the hope that it might suggest something to one of them.

It was a bibliophile who resolved the enigma. *Everhard* might refer to the name of one of the heroes of Jack London, the American writer of adventure stories, in particular to *The Iron Heel*, a political book written in 1907. At last, a 'key' to a code had been found—with some difficulty, because the book was banned in Germany. A copy was found in a library in Bavaria. Unfortunately, however, it only served to decode a certain number of the messages. The rest remained strictly incomprehensible, as if the code had been changed in the meantime.

The Germans realised how admirably this operator protected himself. Not only did he constantly change the wavelengths on which he transmitted his messages, but just as frequently his codes! An almost endless amount of work would have to be done by the SD decoders before any sense could be made of all the other transmissions that had been recorded. However, they had learnt enough to know that the broadcasts dating from January to February 1942 revealed German defence secrets. Moreover, they had obviously been intended for Moscow, since they provided detailed information concerning German troop movements on the eastern front.

These two discoveries, coming within a few days of each other, both delighted and disturbed Walter Schellenberg. This is confirmed by the statements he made to the British after the war. The Wehrmacht was being undermined from within. This was evident from the abundance of detail provided.

Who but German officers would be able to communicate information of such extraordinary value to the Russians? The Russians must have set up an espionage cell among the officer corps—a cell totally independent of the usual networks that had been regularly unmasked by the SD since the discovery of the most important of them, *Die Rote Kapelle*. This network had also been helped by Becker, a brilliant colonel, and by Schulze-Boysen, a lieutenant-colonel in the Luftwaffe, to get military information.

Schellenberg had a vague feeling that something was wrong with his analysis of the situation. If this espionage cell in the Wehrmacht existed, why had the Russians concealed its wireless-operator in Switzerland? He knew only too well how difficult it was to cross the Swiss frontiers. New precautions had to be taken constantly to smuggle his own spies into the Confederation. How could the agents of this supposed cell transmit their news to their technician in Switzerland except by radio? Especially as the transmissions from Switzerland, between January and February 1942, had been almost daily. But if they possessed a transmitter to send their information to their man in Switzerland, why did they not send it directly to Moscow, as *Die Rote Kapelle* had done?

It struck Walter Schellenberg that there could only be one answer: the Swiss had something to do with this affair. They might even be accomplices in it. How far could the Swiss go in their balancing act? Very far indeed, if they showed themselves to be as clever in this field as they had been in organising their supplies in advance. While Europe was wearing wooden shoes and clothes made of cellulose and staple fibre, Swiss shops were full of articles made from pure wool and pure cotton, not to mention the *delicatessen* and the wheaten bread. Who knew what ingenuity they would be capable of to preserve their sacrosanct neutrality!

For a long time Schellenberg had been building up a remarkable espionage organisation which, at the right moment would play a considerable part in overthrowing the Confederation. And now this affair had revealed an unsuspected side to that country. Something had to be done. He must find out what was going on in the heads of the Swiss leaders. To do this, he would have to exercise his customary patience and diplomacy and create an atmosphere of trust.

13

THE GROUND HAD BEEN WELL
prepared for Schellenberg. The coverage of Switzerland by
the German espionage services was more concentrated and
more active than in any other country in the world. This
coverage had begun as early as 1937, as if the Reich had
guessed in advance that any internal opposition to Nazism
would turn first to Switzerland—a fellow German-speaking
state—for refuge.

The German infiltration of Switzerland was entrusted to
two organisations: the Abwehrstelle, the Wehrmacht's
espionage, counter-espionage and sabotage service, under
Admiral Canaris, and the Sicherheitsdienst of Himmler and
Walter Schellenberg. Together, the two organisations had
established branches in Stuttgart, 120 kilometres to the
north of the Confederation, which would deal specifically
with Switzerland.

Lieutenant-Colonel Zeitz had been placed in charge of the
Abwehr office. Lieutenant-Colonel Schmidt, specialising in
military matters, was kept constantly informed about the
Swiss Army. His colleague, Major Gayler, had an up to date

and detailed picture of the Swiss economy. Baron von Stauffenberg, alias Uncle Frank, was in charge of the espionage network itself. He actually sent out more than a thousand agents who infiltrated Swiss industrial and political circles. Major Heiland armed these spies and supplied them with money, false identities, radios, special inks and cameras. Captain Frentznik, known to his colleagues as 'Marconi', was in charge of the transmitter-receiver centre at Sigmaringen, which was used by the organisations covering Switzerland. Four advance posts—at Lörrach, Säckingen, Constance and Bregentz—directed activities near the Swiss frontier.

The office of the Sicherheitsdienst in Stuttgart had 20,000 files on Swiss citizens who could be 'used'. It trained 300 agents every six months, which were then sent into Switzerland to recruit their accomplices. This was done first among Germans living in the Confederation and among the naturalised Swiss, or *papierschweizer*. Frontiersmen of double nationality were also chosen for indoctrination.

The action of the Sicherheitsdienst was of a political nature. When a practical operation was required, the SD called in Heinrich Müller's Gestapo or Otto Skorszeny's Jagdkommando. It was the latter that undertook the first hostile action against Switzerland in 1940. Only the perspicacity of a Swiss railway-worker, on Sunday, June 16, stopped the attempt from taking place.

He was inspecting tickets on the Romanshorn-Zürich train, when he noticed something suspicious: ten passengers, who had got on at Weinfelden and taken up seats in two carriages, had identical brown canvas suit-cases. He informed the police at Märstetten, the next stop. But, alarmed by the insistence with which he had observed them, the ten men jumped from the train.

A search was set up and two days later nine of them were captured, seven Germans and two Swiss. Each possessed 500 Swiss francs, an 'infernal machine' loaded with 2½ kg. of trotyl, a supply of food, tools, a Luger 9 mm revolver with forty cartridges and a dagger.

They were supposed to blow up the ammunition depot at Altdorf, in the canton of Uri and sabotage the runways of the military airfields at Lausanne, Payerne, Bienne and Spreitenbach—an operation ordered by Hermann Goering, as reprisals for four German fighters who had been shot down by anti-aircraft guns while flying over Swiss territory. On November 16, 1940, the nine agents were given life sentences; the tenth had succeeded in getting back to Germany by forcing his way across the frontier at Constance.

Baron von Stauffenberg, the head of the Action section of the Abwehr in Stuttgart had more success in his first attack on Switzerland. At dawn on September 4, 1940, a convoy of cars bearing the emblem of the Red Cross stopped near the Lavillat viaduct, in Haute-Savoie, over which the Annecy-La Roche-sur-Foron railway crossed a ravine. The first car seemed to have had a breakdown. Men were busy under the bonnet. Meanwhile, another group fixed 80 kg. of melinite under one of the pillars of the bridge. The convoy moved on. Some hours later the bridge collapsed.

This bridge was of great value to Switzerland. Since the destruction of the railway at Pontarlier, the tunnel at Frasne and the fine construction of the Bellegarde-Geneva line, Switzerland had used only this line for the transportation of its overseas supplies. For two months, the country had to rely on a shuttle-service of lorries between Annecy and Geneva to link it with the free world.

The missions of the Abwehr and the Sicherheitsdienst ran into thousands. A scale of payment was drawn up: 1,000 Swiss francs for the empty shell of an anti-tank grenade; 1,500 if full; reports on the national defence programme, 1,500; with photographs, 2,000; weapons or new projectiles, up to 50,000. This had already enabled the OKW to publish in 1940 a small work of eighty-five pages, entitled *Handbook of the Swiss Army*, intended for the use of German troops in the event of a possible invasion of the country.

To force the frontiers, the Germans used two techniques. A few hundred metres away from the chosen place, they created a diversion, firing shots as if in pursuit of someone. This drew the attention of the customs officers and frontier guards and left the field free for the spies. Passers-by who hid them were paid 1,000 francs per agent.

The second method was safer, but more expensive: 1,500 francs. The crossing took place in Basle railway-station. The German customs officers took the spies, disguised as railway-workers, across the lines and handed them over to their Swiss accomplices. Basle station, an international junction between Switzerland, Germany and France was, throughout the war, more frequented by spies than perhaps any other single place in the world. Colonel Jaquillard, head of Swiss counter-espionage, was to count with stupefaction 350 known German spies on the nights of May 14 and 15, 1940, alone. They were sitting quietly, on the German side of the frontier, awaiting the best time to slip into Switzerland.

Throughout the war, the SD never ceased their efforts to win over the Swiss to Nazism. With this aim in view, a Bureau 'F' had been set up in Berne: this was a cell for recruitment and subversion. The Consul-General, Hans Meisner, directed this cell which was concealed in the German legation. It included a group of well-trained specialists who, like Meisner, benefited from their diplomatic immunity.

By the middle of 1942, the number of Germans living in Switzerland had almost reached the proportions of a state within a state. Brigadier Masson did not underestimate the gravity of this situation. He often exceeded his annual budget of 50 million Swiss francs, without causing too much opposition, but the means at his disposal in terms of men and money were hardly adequate to withstand the Nazi tide. He congratulated himself on having persuaded the local police forces, as early as 1938, to keep a special register of foreign residents in every locality. For each name in this register there was an arrest-warrant, made out in advance. At the slightest sign of suspicion, his agents struck. Between 1939 and 1942, they had had no fewer than a thousand calls. Not all of these turned out to be genuine cases, of course—

and occasionally an innocent person was incriminated.

By the middle of 1942, however, Masson's service had become so efficient that the best spies began to fall into their nets. The Germans never gave their men more than three months activity in Switzerland. This led them to change their tactics. Since their networks seemed to be so short-lived, they decided to practise the technique of *uberschwem-mung*, or inundation. If one agent disappeared, he would be replaced by five.

To this, the Swiss replied by increasing the severity of their penalties. Espionage had not so far been treated very harshly by the Federal Courts. Indeed, they had often been content to expel the 'undesirables'. The courts were now ordered to act ruthlessly. More than 1,500 spies, including fifty women, were charged with activities against the security of the Swiss state. Two hundred and two were given sentences of between five and fifteen years—among them were sixty-four Germans, sixteen citizens of Liechtenstein and 164 Swiss. Thirty-three spies were given life sentences and nineteen were condemned to death, sixteen of these being executed.

This, then, was the situation in Switzerland when SS-Brigadeführer Walter Schellenberg was trying to work out how he could tackle Switzerland in a new, subtler and more profitable way.

14

SCHELLENBERG DECIDED TO
aim high—at no less a person than Brigadier Roger Masson
himself. A year and a half before, on Schellenberg's orders,
one of his most talented adjutants, SS-Sturmbannführer
H. W. Eggen, had begun to prepare the ground. As we
have seen, Eggen had succeeded in building up close
relations with two Swiss wood merchants. His choice of
these two men was a deliberate one: before meeting them,
Eggen knew that Captains Meyer and Holzach were among
Masson's closest colleagues.

From the beginning of the war, Walter Schellenberg had
planned to meet Roger Masson, hoping to establish 'friendly'
relations with him. Such a contact could always be useful—
it would give him easy access into Switzerland, for example,
and enable him to place gold and hard currency in a bank,
under an anonymous number. And, who knows, he might
even succeed in persuading the Confederation not to resist
the Wehrmacht, if Hitler were suddenly to decide to annexe
the German-speaking parts of Switzerland.

Since then, Schellenberg's objectives had changed considerably. And this meeting, which so far Roger Masson had obstinately avoided, despite a number of attempts made by Eggen to interest Meyer and Holzach, had now become urgent. In fact, with implacable logic, Schellenberg had analysed his problem thoroughly.

Reinhard Heydrich had thought that the traitors who were informing the Russians were to be found among the officers of the Wehrmacht. At this time, the end of June 1942, the SS-Brigadeführer was still convinced that these officers were being helped by the traditional opposition to Hitler. He thought at once of Admiral Canaris, then of the head of the Abwehr network in Switzerland, Hans Bernd Gisevius, the Vice-Consul.

Only one person could help him to ascertain whether the usual conspirators in Berlin were also involved in this affair —Colonel Masson. This was why he wished to meet him. He did not, of course, hope to find an ally. He would try to strangle Switzerland in a tight net of obligations. He did not lack ammunition for this. Only when he felt that the Swiss secret service chief had been well and truly hooked, would he reveal his true intentions. If the Swiss really were unaware of this affair—which still seemed quite possible— then Schellenberg would quite simply ask for their help in destroying these enemies of Nazism.

As yet, the SS-Brigadeführer felt that he lacked one thing. He would have liked to have begun this game of power with an ace up his sleeve. Unwittingly, Colonel Masson was to present him with just such a card.

Among the dispatches concerning Switzerland that reached him twice a week from the office of his Sicherheitsdienst in Stuttgart, Schellenberg found a piece of information which, although apparently innocent enough, set up a long train of thought in his fertile brain. A young Swiss lieutenant had just arrived in Stuttgart: a new employee in the chancellery of the Swiss consulate. It was his first post. It wouldn't be very difficult to have him watched. For it was a well-known fact that employees of embassies and consulates were often used to carry out 'information' missions. This lieutenant was called Möergeli.

An hour later, Schellenberg rang SS-Sturmbannführer Hügel, the head of the Stuttgart office, and ordered him to mount a *Herausforderung*, or provocation, intended for young Möergeli. When arrested, he was to be given the full treatment. A tribunal would give him the maximum penalty for espionage activities. His consul and the Swiss authorities would certainly intervene—which was just what he wanted. He hoped in this way to force Roger Masson to come to Germany.

Meanwhile, on the eastern front, the artillery had opened fire once more. For four hours the Russian lines were bombarded, as a preparation for the launching of 'Operation Blue', which, it was hoped, would be the Wehrmacht's final, victorious onslaught on the Red Army.

For a long time Hitler had hesitated to give the green light to his troop commanders, Field Marshal von Bock and General Friedrich Paulus. A Fieseler Storch, a small reconnaissance plane, had been shot down eight days before in a sector held by the Russians, near the banks of the Oskol, east of Kharkov. In the plane was an officer of the 23rd Tank Division, Major Reichel. In Reichel's brief-case there were notes and maps indicating the positions of the divisions and the objectives of the whole of the 40th Tank Corps. Field Marshal Keitel timidly suggested to the Führer that the offensive be delayed, for the Russians would certainly be in possession of a large part of the Wehrmacht's plans. Von Bock and Paulus protested:

"Even if the Russians possess the plans of the 40th Corps, which is not yet certain, they will not have time to arrange their defences accordingly. Moreover, the 40th Corps will only cover part of the front. The rest of the plans remain strictly secret. Lastly, if we delay our enterprise now, it will never have a chance of success. It will be winter before we have attained our objectives."

Despite the lesson of Moscow, Hitler seems to have followed the advice of the timorous Wilhelm Keitel—in the hope, perhaps, that his scientists, working under Wernher von Braun, would not be long in providing him with their super-rockets capable of subjugating the world.

But, of course, the Russians knew not only the plans of the 40th Armoured Corps—though it would appear that they had found nothing in the wreckage of the Fieseler Storch—they had full details also of the whole of 'Operation Blue', the code name of the second massive attack in 1942.

Despite his dexterity, which had come to him through endless practice in the service of the Russians, Foote, Rado's chief operator in Lausanne, had great difficulty in communicating this enormous pile of coded dispatches to the 'Centre'. Every night he spent five hours coding the heap of messages that piled up on his desk. His difficulties were not attenuated by the frequent changes of coding ordered by Moscow. Then, from 1 a.m., the silence of his room was broken by the remorseless tapping of his transmitter. With the windows carefully sealed to prevent any light from showing outside, he sat there until dawn, the air becoming thicker and thicker from the smoke of his innumerable cigarettes.

Rudolf Roessler had communicated his contagious ardour to the whole of Rado's network. Foote was no longer able to cope with the sheer quantity of 'Lucy's' messages and Margareta Bolli and Edmund Hamel were put on to the transmission of the 'WYRDO', or messages of maximum priority. There was a particular reason for the sudden increase in the volume of work being put through this network: for the first time since they had begun to use the services of this exceptional secret agent, whom they did not know, the Russians had made radical changes in their strategy.

Until then they had been content, thanks to their information, to make perfect estimates of the forces and the plans of the enemy. But when the battles took place, they ignored the further use to which 'Lucy's' information could be put, and fought according to the academic rules they had learnt in their military schools from their teachers in the 'black'

Reichswehr. Knowing everything about the fate that awaited them, they allowed themselves, almost fatalistically, to meet the enemy on the ground and at the times determined by the Germans. An analysis of the tactics used during the first year of the conflict shows quite clearly that although the Russians knew exactly what the Germans planned to do, they almost always allowed themselves to be encircled and pinned down. The result was a horrible, inexplicable holocaust. However, from 1942 things were to go differently.

From then on the Red Army was to elude the Wehrmacht. It learnt to escape from all the pincer-movements that had worked so successfully before. It continued to attack and defend from a frontal position, but it suddenly adopted tactics involving great mobility. It no longer defended positions with exaggerated doggedness, but drew the German troops into terrain that was not suited to the broad formations required by armoured divisions. It was now the Red Army that had captured the initiative; it was they who decided the times and the places of battles. Moreover, it was the Russians who introduced a new weapon into the war—one that was to be much used later on—psychological warfare. This consisted of a mixture of information and threats. It was the 2nd Hungarian Army that became its first victim. In the middle of the night, it was addressed by voices coming from powerful loud-speakers just within the Russian lines:

"Hungarians! We know that tomorrow, at dawn, you will cross the Oskol. But we shall not be there to meet you. We shall meet when and where *we* wish. You will then be sorry you ever came to Russia. You will curse your leaders for having given in to Field Marshal Keitel and agreeing to send you here."

The 23rd Tank Division, which had previously been stationed in France and which had only just arrived on the eastern front was greeted by this message:

"Soldiers of the 23rd. Welcome to the Soviet Union! Your fine Paris days are over now. What awaits you in our country will far surpass anything your comrades, who were frost-bitten, may have told you. But you will see for your-selves before long!"

The 24th Tank Division also received these nocturnal addresses over loud-speakers:

"Panzergrenadiers of the 24th, we shall not be south of Voronezh the day after tomorrow as your leaders have said. You needn't try and encircle us—we won't be there. Save your bread, your ammunition and your petrol. For we are going to besiege you. The luckiest among you will be those who have kept a bullet to blow their own brains out."

This new use by the Russians of a minute part of the information provided by 'Lucy' appears implicitly in a great many of the German soldiers' accounts of the cam-paign. The same feeling of insecurity recurs in all these accounts—a feeling that is to be found in descriptions of the actions on no other front. The combatants on the eastern front got the disastrous impression that the enemy had access to the plans of their chiefs. They became paralysed by a feeling that the red terror would engulf them in the middle of the inhospitable steppes. The first attempt by the Russians at using this technique was an unqualified success.

It had a particular effect on the ordinary soldiers, even to the extent of causing mental breakdowns. The officers of the Wehrmacht tended to make fun of it, but in a sense they were even more affected since they realised that the Russians possessed other, much more valuable information, that they did not broadcast from their loud-speakers, but which would enable them at the front to overthrow completely the usual tactics of the OKW.

These mid-months of 1942 also marked a new stage for Roger Masson and the Bureau Ha in their relations with Roessler. They began to feel that Roessler had changed—and the change was not to their liking. When, in 1939, on the recommendation of Xavier Schnieper, they had begun using him, their attitude towards him was not devoid of a certain condescension. By some extraordinary chance, they thought, this émigré had access to a source of information whose importance he did not himself appear to realise.

So they used him—for their own ends, then in the interests of the western Allies, whom, they believed, represented the same ideals as themselves. When this curious individual announced that he also wanted to work for the Russians, who had now joined the Allies, they turned a blind eye to the matter, fully expecting that it would not lead to very much.

With the first great Russian victories—'his' victories, he had an irritating habit of calling them—Roessler seemed to become a 'bigger' person, or perhaps simply to reveal his true nature. He may not have been interested in money, but he seemed strangely affected by feelings of power and pride. This new Roessler, who, they now realised, was the real head of his resistance network, suddenly became dangerous.

However, he continued to fulfil the conditions agreed between them. He made no attempt to conceal from them the information he passed on to the Russians. But Roger Masson and the Bureau Ha realised that, by means of this information, he would play an overwhelming rôle in the victory of the Russians in the East. If, by some misfortune, the Germans discovered that it was thanks to Switzerland this had been possible, then the neutrality of the Confederation would be in jeopardy. The very existence of Switzerland as an independent state might be in danger.

From then on, few men except leading statesmen, were to be as closely guarded as Roessler. Night and day, the Vita Nova Verlag, in the Fluhmattstrasse, in Lucerne, and his home at Wesemlin were 'watched' by huge, shadowy, scrupulously discreet figures. If Roessler was aware of them, he did not show it—and he expressed no gratitude for this protection. This irritated the Swiss.

One particularly warm night, at the end of this summer of 1942, the wireless-operator at Geneva airport was feeling bored. The Swiss air force made no flights after nightfall, but the authorities insisted that someone should remain at the radio controls throughout the night. After wandering aimlessly around his office the operator sat down at his instruments. He began to play idly with the knobs. Suddenly, he intercepted a broadcast on a wavelength that was not used by the Swiss armed forces. The letters and figures appeared in groups of five. From the touch, it sounded like an amateur. The operator tried to understand the message. Failing to do so, he informed BUPO, the Swiss counter-espionage service. He had made a note of the wavelength and the time of the broadcast. The clandestine transmitter was quite near the airport, probably in Geneva itself, for throughout the transmission the tone had been extremely sharp and clear. Moreover, the strength of the transmission meant that the set was using the local electricity supply and not batteries.

The following night, three vans, equipped with 'gonios' waited near the airport and picked up the same transmission that had begun again. It was coming from the south-east. They set out slowly from three different points, and guided by the sound began to converge on a point in the centre of Geneva. When the tapping stopped, at almost the same time as the previous night, the van had already crossed the bridges over the Rhône. The next night they got even closer to the clandestine transmitter. One of the gonios was near the university, the second was in the rue Versonnex beside the Jardin Anglais, and the third near the Parc de la Grange.

On the fourth day of the search, they intercepted a new transmitter, in the same direction. This set also seemed to be manipulated by an amateur, but a clumsier one than the other. They then lost touch with the broadcasts. A week later, the gonio vans were stationed in the route de Florissant, at the gates of the Parc Alfred Bertrand, when the tapping began again. This time it was so strong that the technicians were in no doubt that the operator must be somewhere in that street.

A single gonio did the final work of tracking down. To locate the actual house from which the operator was broadcasting, the BUPO agents had recourse to a trick which had been invented by the Germans. The electric current of each house was cut in turn, just long enough for a man to walk from one to the next. If the broadcast continued, then the secret operator was in the house in front of which they were passing. In this way they eventually located the house as number 192, route de Florissant.

The same method tracked down the second transmitter to 8 bis, rue Henri Mussard. It was now child's play for Brigadier Masson's department to put names to the street numbers. Both were on the lists of suspect persons because they both belonged to the Swiss Communist Party: Edmond Hamel and Margareta Bolli.

A Swiss coding expert, Marc Payot, set to work, without great enthusiasm, to 'break' the enigmatic dispatches recorded since the discovery of these transmissions. The Swiss counter-espionage agents were less interested in what these communists might be communicating as in the fact that they had continuous relations with a correspondent outside the Confederation. It seemed obvious to them that this correspondent could only be Moscow—and that Hamel and Bolli must be Roessler's wireless-operators.

The couple were carefully watched and the results confirmed this theory. Hamel and Bolli both paid frequent visits to a certain Rado, who also received in his office at the Géo-Presse a certain Christian Schneider, a close friend of Rudolf Roessler. These discoveries came as a great relief to Roger Masson and the Bureau Ha: at last they had a way of blocking the work of this frighteningly effective agent if the need arose. They could destroy him as easily as they could defend him.

The reason for this sudden mistrust of Roessler was due not to any real change in the information Roessler received, but rather in the use to which it was being put by the Russians. But to understand the fears experienced by the Swiss at that time we should take another look at events on the eastern front.

On July 1, 1942, the Wehrmacht started moving once more from the positions it had won in May. The first objective was Voronezh, an economic and industrial centre and a road and rail junction. The Germans had planned to make Voronezh the fortress that would cover the Wehrmacht's offensive on its north flank. Three German and one Hungarian army would cross the Oskil, with General Hoth's tanks as their spear-head.

The first surprise for the German troops was that the six Soviet armies, under Semyon Konstantinovich Timoshenko, which they had expected to encircle from the north and the south, had disappeared without engaging battle and it was not certain which direction they had taken. Feeling that their attack had now been inexplicably blunted, the Wehrmacht officers wished to abandon 'Operation Blue' altogether and pursue the Russian on a wide front in the direction of the Don. Hitler refused: they must first encircle the Russians. Terrified in advance of leaving the initiative to his High Command, the Führer stuck obstinately to his own plans.

On July 3, General Hoth's 4th Army and Friedrich Paulus's 6th Army joined up as planned. But there was nothing there. The huge net they had spread was empty. Hitler realised that the Russians had outwitted him. On a lightning visit to von Bock's headquarters, he went into a violent rage: "I'm not interested in Voronezh any more! Go south and get Stalingrad."

He did not say he did not *want* Voronezh. Completely baffled and fearing that he might be reproached later with not following 'Directive 41' to the letter, von Bock temporised. Without knowing it he was being lured on by Timoshenko, who had allowed the 24th Tank Division to forge on unopposed to within a few kilometres of Voronezh. Meanwhile Timoshenko was admirably informed as to the doubts, expectations and movements of the German forces by an ever more effective 'Lucy'.

At this period, in fact, which lasted for more than a month, scarcely *ten hours* elapsed between the taking of a decision by the OKW and the reception of this decision by Moscow. On one occasion, the interval was reduced to six hours. Roessler had calculated rightly that only speed in the transmission of this news would enable the Kremlin to develop a strategy which, in the course of the decisive battle, would turn the war in their favour. And the Russians who were only too well aware of this, never had occasion to ask 'Lucy' to accelerate the supply of information.

On July 4, von Bock believed that he could take Voronezh in a surprise attack. He remained convinced that Timoshenko's troops could only have escaped from the trap by going south and north and that they had not yet crossed the Don. Moreover, this was proved by the fact that the bridges were intact. It did not occur to him for a moment that this might be a trap.

"And what's happening to the attack in the south?" Hitler asked.

"Contingents of the 24th Division are already entering the outskirts of the city. The Russians are fleeing," von Bock replied.

This time it was Hitler himself who fell right into the trap. He ordered that the troops should be split up. About half, including the 6th Army, would set out for Stalingrad in the south—but they would make no attempt to take the city, their mission being to by-pass the Soviet armies. As soon as von Bock had occupied Voronezh he was to continue straight on and link up with Paulus. This time the Russians would not escape their net and they would be duly destroyed. The second branch of the pincer-movement would simply arrive a little after the first.

On receiving this news from 'Lucy', Timoshenko was exultant. The Germans were making a serious mistake in dividing their strike-force. The Soviet High Command could not have wished for a more favourable situation. In fact, the full use to which the information from *Werther* and *Olga* was being put enabled the Russians to work out a system of implacable tactics: break the striking force of the Wehrmacht, then lure a large body of troops into a cul-de-sac where they could be wiped out. Meanwhile, the second body of troops was to be contained in a place that was suitable for long drawn-out combat, thus preventing it from going to the rescue of the first column and linking up to form another group of armies which would be difficult to defeat. The cul-de-sac would be Stalingrad and the battle-field Voronezh!

In answer to 'Operation Blue', therefore, Timoshenko, like von Bock, divided his forces. But they were more numerous and better supplied with fuel than the Germans, because they held the railways. So the larger section of the Soviet troops awaited the advance of Paulus's 6th Army, harassing it constantly, without pinning it down and gradually cutting it off from its rear lines. Meanwhile, the rest of the troops, under Timoshenko himself, waited in Voronezh, possessing far more artillery than von Bock expected to meet.

When the German general ordered the city to be taken, the time of disillusion for the Third Reich had sounded. It was a foretaste of the catastrophe to come. In their accounts, von Bock's officers nicknamed Voronezh 'the cursed city'. They fought their way through the suburbs only to come to a standstill in the centre of the city—but the outcome of the fighting never seemed clear. It was impossible for them to withdraw—they had got in too far for their departure not to look like a defeat.

But Timoshenko did get out of the city. He left Voronezh at just the moment he wished and, without leaving a single lorry behind, disappeared into the steppe. He withdrew when the mass of troops that he had sent in the direction of Stalingrad to open the way for Paulus's 6th Army had reached the Volga. These troops were eighteen days ahead of the Germans. Realising one morning that Paulus was no longer following him, the general in command sent word to Moscow asking whether the Germans had changed their plans.

The 'Centre' alerted Foote, who passed on the message to Roessler. The incredible reply from 'Lucy' caused much rejoicing among the Russians. Paulus's 6th Army had run out of petrol and would be immobilised for 430 hours. This unexpected respite allowed the future defenders of Stalingrad to reinforce their lines.

On the Caucasian front, too, the Russians applied the new

tactics, being able, thanks to 'Lucy's' timely warnings to evade all the numerous attempts at encirclement made by Field Marshal Siegmund Wilhelm List. The commanding officers engaged in 'Operation Blue' were to discover, too late, that what they had interpreted as retreats were, in fact, concerted withdrawals, which in time were to seal the fate of the Third Reich.

By the beginning of September these officers were to realise with consternation that their armies, scattered over the four corners of the horizon, separated from each other by sometimes as much as 500 kilometres, linked by lines of communications that were stretched to breaking-point, had become terribly vulnerable. Sunk in the sand of the steppe, surrounded by wide, open spaces, the Wehrmacht's wonderful strike-force no longer existed. The Red Army, aided by the oncoming winter, would be able to destroy it at leisure. The situation was a brilliant success on the part of the Soviet High Command—though a large share of the credit should go to 'Lucy', without whom it would never have been possible.

Through his notorious inability to understand, let alone solve, large-scale strategic problems, Hitler was also an involuntary accomplice of the Russians.

"They're finished, they're exhausted," he cried contemptuously to General Halder, his chief of staff, who dared to convey to him the fears of his troops on the eastern front. "Can't you see that Russia is finished? Stalin will never be able, as you claim, to mobilise 1,500,000 fresh men for Stalingrad, not to mention the 500,000 he is supposed to be launching on the Caucasus. I forbid you to go on repeating such nonsense!"

He even withdrew troops from this sector of the Russian front, sending seven precious divisions to France, via Leningrad. It is impossible to say, with any certainty, whether they would have succeeded in withstanding the Russian tide that was to sweep over the troops of List and Paulus.

In any case, these were the first results of the information conveyed at that time to Stalin by 'Lucy'. It helps one to understand the anxiety felt by the Swiss secret service. It was of the utmost importance that Hitler should learn nothing of the part played by Switzerland in this affair.

In Berlin, however, one person had coldly analysed the development of events from July to September on the eastern front: Walter Schellenberg. He alone among the leading Nazis understood the part that was being played by the resistance network he was trying to track down. It was becoming more and more urgent for him to strike before this leak did any further damage to the Reich. On Monday, September 7, 1942, five days after the decision taken 2,500 kilometres away by Friedrich Paulus to attack Stalingrad, he set out in his blue Mercedes for the banks of the Rhine, accompanied by SS-Sturmbannführer H. W. Eggen. He had Roger Masson in a trap. The next day, they would meet at Waldshut. Even if it failed, it was worth trying to save Nazism.

15

WALTER SCHELLENBERG'S
first meeting with Roger Masson in September 1942 gave
the SS-Brigadeführer great satisfaction. He had found a
man who was obviously under great tension. He had been
expecting this, of course, having done everything possible
to cause it.

Masson had laid down one condition to his accepting the
meeting. It must take place in a town on the German-Swiss
border, Laufenburg, for example. So Schellenberg decided
to 'condition' Masson a little before arriving himself. He
invented a motor accident. He needed a serious hold-up that
would justify changing the place of the meeting to somewhere further inside Germany—to Waldshut. It is easier to
beat an opponent on home ground. Moreover, the delay
should be long enough for a Gestapo agent to augment the
feeling of insecurity already instilled into the guest by being
suddenly plunged into hostile surroundings.

Although the members of the Gestapo were hardly noted
for their finesse, the mission was performed to Schellenberg's satisfaction. He had found a Masson who had been

put off balance. He took advantage of this situation to disconcert the Swiss officer even more, by making apparently gratuitous concessions. He was to make a great many more before asking the crucial question as to whether he knew who was betraying the Wehrmacht.

The head of the Swiss information service was certainly worried. He must not be allowed to regain his calm. As Masson had begun to be in Schellenberg's debt, he could hardly refuse further interviews. He must be enticed further into the net and suffocated by progressively greater debts. If, in the end, he still refused to co-operate then he could be destroyed.

This plan had only one, but very serious, defect—it needed time. And time was Germany's most precious commodity. Things were happening quickly on the eastern front. This convinced the SS-Brigadeführer that the Russians were still receiving providential information in abundance —information that enabled them, always in time, to evade whatever traps the Wehrmacht might lay for them.

On September 2, 1942, for example: at a distance of about forty kilometres from Stalingrad was an imposing belt of fortifications that blocked any access to the city. This line would take a great many men and too much material and ammunition if attacked head on. To the west, there was the Don; to the east, the Volga; the south, the Karpovka. Parallel to the Don, hills overlooked the Rossochka, a stream compared with the other great rivers. The summits of these natural obstacles were highly fortified—in guns and men.

At the foot of these hill fortresses, Paulus and his 6th Army waited, hesitant. Hoth was coming from the south, from the Caucasus, with the 48th Tank Division, a number of infantry divisions and the Rumanians of the 6th Corps. On that side, too, hills preceded the steppe of the Kalmuks, broken by a few ravines that led to Stalingrad. However, there was one weak spot in this defence system—the little town of Gavrilovka. It was there that Hoth wanted to make his break-through. If he got through he would take the

Russians from behind. Paulus could then attack and the Russians would be caught in the classic encirclement so dear to the Wehrmacht strategists. The OKW agreed to the manoeuvre and the troops moved into action.

On September 2, 1942, in the early hours of the morning, German reconnaissance patrols signalled that the Russians had abandoned the positions in which they should have been annihilated. They had disappeared—as if two days before they had been reading, over the shoulders of Hoth and Paulus, the telegram from the OKW approving the plan. None the less, he gave orders for the advance to go on. Eremenko and Zhukov were waiting for him, on the outskirts of Stalingrad, in a place that made the encirclement impossible. He would lose the battle, but he did not know that yet.

For Schellenberg, this and many other episodes since the beginning of 'Operation Blue' confirmed his doubts. Even if they had been unable to discover new codes used by the people they were trying to track down among the mass of intercepted and recorded dispatches, at least his listening service at Dresden had confirmed that clandestine broadcasts coming from Switzerland were continuing without interruption—from Switzerland, where the members of the opposition to the Führer plotted together and kept up unnumerable contacts with the enemies of the Reich, particularly with the western Allies. This had just been proved by a recent incident.

At the beginning of the autumn, 1942, the Gestapo arrested a Munich businessman called Schmidthuber. He was suspected of smuggling foreign currency into Switzerland. Under pressure, administered by the SD, he suddenly revealed that he worked for the Abwehr of Admiral Canaris and that he was taking the money on his orders. Investigations showed that Schmidthuber had not been lying. Schellenberg's Bureau 'F' in Berne also undertook a lightning inquiry in the Confederation.

The currency the man had been carrying was intended for a group of Jewish refugees. The Abwehr supporting Jews!

This was about the worst crime a Nazi could conceive. Realising that the little admiral would never get himself out of the trap into which he had fallen, Schmidthuber talked, hoping at least to save his own head. He denounced Canaris, who, he said, was guilty of trying to negotiate a peace with the British. The admiral's first attempt had been negotiated through the Vatican as early as December 1939. He revealed the names of the accomplices: Colonel Hans Oster, Judge Hans von Dohnanyi, Oberleutnant Josef Müller and others, who were later executed by the SS.

However, even Schellenberg had connections of this kind with the British, through a batman called Jahnke, mentioned earlier. But he never hoped to need them—he intended them simply as an emergency exit, in the unthinkable event of Hitler being deserted by fortune. If the opponents of the Führer were capable of betraying Germany to the West, they could just as easily do so to the East. This is what strengthened Schellenberg's original conviction that the traitors he was looking for were to be found among the traditional opposition.

After the Schmidthuber affair, Schellenberg left Wilhelm Canaris no freedom. Even when he had become certain that the admiral had no part in the extraordinary case he was studying, he continued to have him watched, urged on perhaps by a sadistic desire to hasten the admiral's fall. He spied on him constantly, even to the point of accompanying him on his riding excursions in the Berlin suburbs. It was Schellenberg himself who arrested Canaris in 1944, and who drove him in his own black Mercedes convertible to Fürstenberg, where he handed him over to SS-Brigadeführer Trummler, a colleague of his. He then took over the job as head of the Abwehr, which he incorporated into his own 4th and 6th counter-espionage bureaux. Schellenberg was not convinced that Canaris and his fellow-conspirators in Switzerland were innocent of the major, permanent communication of military information to the Russians until November 1942, that is, a month after his second meeting with Colonel Masson, at Wolfsberg, Captain Meyer's house at Ermatingen.

Schellenberg had surpassed himself during that long weekend in Switzerland from October 16 to 18, 1942. He had used his histrionic powers to the full. He had told his hosts the story of his life. He had also indulged in one of his favourite sins: attributing the aims of others—in this case those of Canaris and his group—to himself. He let his listeners understand that he was concerned about the way the war was going, that he would be willing to serve as an intermediary between Germany and the western Allies, with a view to negotiating a compromise peace. He also hinted at the possibility of forming a common front, after such a peace, against Bolshevism. He had hoped to get some reaction out of Masson. But the brigadier's face had remained utterly expressionless. The Swiss intelligence chief was not proving quite so easy to manipulate as Schellenberg had thought at first. When he returned to Berlin, the head of the Sicherheitsdienst reflected for a long time on the suitability of his tactics. Should he continue to play with the Swiss? A month later an event occurred that persuaded him that he would soon have to show his claws. This event was the sudden appearance in broad daylight of Allen Dulles.

The grandson of an American missionary in India, Dulles had attended the Ecole Alsacienne, in Paris, before going on to Princeton. He then became a school teacher, first in India, then in China. In 1916, he joined the diplomatic service—or rather the secret service. As early as 1917 he was spying on Austria and Germany from Berne. When, in December 1941, President Roosevelt appointed Major-General William J. Donovan as head of the office of Strategic Service, it was quite natural for Donovan to ask Dulles to work with him.

By November 1942, Allen Dulles was in Berne and had begun work there and in Zürich shortly after the Allied landing in Morocco and Algeria. In fact, only the Swiss authorities knew when he had crossed the frontiers of the

Confederation. In any case, he did so some time before November, since he entered Switzerland from the 'free zone' of France. Unofficial sources have suggested that he had been in the country since the spring of 1942.

No one suspected that a special envoy from Roosevelt—one who enjoyed the full confidence of the President—had been operating all this time incognito in Switzerland. This anonymity enabled him to get a more exact idea of the people who might be able to help him. First, he could depend on complete, unconditional support from the Swiss themselves. General Guisan, Brigadier Masson and the whole Swiss secret service agreed to co-operate with him and the American government. He had also approached a number of French resistance workers, who had agreed to support him and act as 'sources'.

But Dulles wanted more than that: he wanted to gain the co-operation of Germans—not any Germans, but the representatives of a true, sincere opposition to Nazism. He soon discovered that the Swiss were working with such a group and he tried to by-pass the Swiss in order to work with them himself. It might be said that this was the only thing the Swiss refused him. However they revealed to him eventually that they worked with only one member of this network, the head himself, who had been living in Switzerland for a long time. They knew nothing, of course, about *Werther* and *Olga*.

It was then that Allen Dulles decided to announce his intentions to the world. Within a very short time his house in the Herrengasse in Zürich, his flat in the Schweizerhof, on the banks of the 'Lake of the Four Cantons', in Lucerne, and his flat in the Jubiläumsstrasse, in Berne, became highly frequented places.

Dulles had failed to contact the opposition to Hitler by secret means, so he now hoped they would come and contact him. Strangely enough, some of them, the less serious, did—as if the Gestapo or the Sicherheitsdienst did not exist in Switzerland. The first to come forward was Hans Bernd Gisevius, the enormous German Vice-Consul in

Zürich, an ex-police administrator from the early days of Nazism, the permanent special envoy of Canaris and the Abwehr in the Confederation. It was then that Walter Schellenberg abandoned his earlier theory. The men he was trying to track down could never work for the Russians and also for the Americans, who never made any secret of their violent anti-communism.

Gisevius and Dulles met frequently, almost daily at critical periods. The German's mission was to communicate to the Americans messages from General Ludwig Beck and Carl Goerdeler, the minds behind the conspiracy that organised the July 20, 1944, attempt on Hitler's life, and to keep the United States informed about plots against Hitler.

At first, Gisevius tried to conceal his visits to Dulles. One evening, as they were dining together in Berne, Dulles's cook, who did not yet know the Vice-Consul, noticed that the two men were speaking in German. She looked inside the guest's hat and found his initials: H.B.G. That night, she informed the German embassy. Two days later, when Gisevius went to his embassy on routine business he was accused of treason by two senior officials. The Vice-Consul rounded on them furiously. Of course he visited Dulles—and he had an excellent reason for doing so. Dulles was quite simply his best espionage source among the Allies. He added that if the two officials wished to keep their jobs they had better forget what they had just heard. Dulles thus learnt that his cook was a Nazi spy and Gisevius learnt that a secret agent never had his initials on his hat band.

Compared with the activities of Rudolf Roessler and his friends, this conspiracy looks pretty childish. It is simply a good illustration of the extraordinary atmosphere of Switzerland at the time. Almost everyone appeared to be working for some secret service or other—or gave the impression that he was. This, of course, provided an admirable smoke screen for the few really important agents. If the game he played with Gisevius seems puerile, Dulles himself was not. He had a difficult task in persuading all the plotting generals around Beck and Canaris, who all wanted a separate peace (and who sometimes suggested the craziest plans for disposing of Hitler), that Britain and the United States would never turn on the Soviet Union while the war continued. For example, Beck suggested the following plan, which he had communicated to Dulles through Gisevius:

"The British and Americans land in western Europe. The German generals then send all their troops west to meet the attack. The western Allies then send three divisions of paratroopers to land on Berlin, to help the plotters hold the capital. Meanwhile, dependable anti-Nazi troops are sent to seize Hitler in his mountain hide-out in the Obersalzberg. The war then continues against the Russians."

These German convulsions, which he carefully analysed, enabled Dulles to conclude that the divergences between the Wehrmacht and the Nazi Party on the one hand, and the SS and Gestapo on the other, would bring about the downfall of Germany just as surely as Hitler's madness. He also learnt, with obvious contempt, that all senior German officers could be bought; all that was necessary was to make an accurate estimate of their price so as not to waste money.

This cruel judgement on the utter amorality of the German war lords, acquired through numerous receptions and secret meetings, explains why Dulles never expected to see his various negotiations really succeed, whether with Himmler, General Wolff and the SS, through their envoy, Prince Max Egon von Hohenlohe, or those with Ludwig Beck and von Bock.

However, his sudden emergence in November 1942 had one result he could not have been aware of. As soon as Walter Schellenberg learnt from his agents in Berne and Zürich, that Gisevius, one of his favourite suspects, was flirting with the Americans, the SS-Brigadeführer reconsidered his problem. Since the men he was looking for no longer seemed to be found among the usual plotters, he would come down on the Swiss.

Anything seemed possible. The Confederation might be

totally unaware that the Russians were using its territory as a wireless-telegraphic relay-station. But it was equally possible that this tiny nation might be running an espionage network which had its roots at the heart of the Reich, in Berlin. There was only one tactic to find out: a trap had to be laid—a trap such as he excelled at elaborating. It was in December 1942 that he hit on an idea for a trap.

Meanwhile, in Stalingrad, the myth of the invincibility of the Wehrmacht was collapsing. Since November 23, Batov, Zhukov, Eremenko and Rokossovski had encircled Paulus and his 6th Army—aided by the invaluable information 'Lucy' transmitted. The Germans had already lost 140,000 men out of 400,000 in front of Stalingrad.

As 'Lucy' had predicted, both to the Russians and to the Bureau Ha, the Italian, Hungarian and Rumanian legions spread out over the 550 kilometres separating Voronezh from Stalingrad had not held their ground. Their lines had been broken and their defences had crumbled. It was there that the Russian grip had tightened inexorably to the west of Paulus's troops. One last, slender hope remained: the 6th, 17th and 23rd Tank Divisions under Hoth, which had gone south to the Caucasus, were returning at full speed and would attempt to break the formidable pressure from the Red Army. Paulus was to be ready to make a breakthrough. Only an element of surprise could win the day.

This element was lacking, thanks to 'Lucy'. Moscow was kept informed of the advance of Hoth's three divisions, on their degree of freshness and on the morale among the troops. They were beginning to show signs of exhaustion. They made a stop at Vassilievka, hardly fifty kilometres from their goal—petrol was running out and new supplies had been held up a hundred kilometres away. The Russians chose this moment, this pause before the planned German attack. The 51st and 67th Armies and the whole of Group 2 hurled themselves on the German tanks and decimated them. Hoth retreated, beaten. There was no more hope for Paulus. Hitler abandoned him, conferring on him the rank of Field Marshal. He was not told this, of course. On the contrary, he was informed that a rescue force, formed at Kharkov, was on its way from the west.

From the west news came of nothing but death, administered by the Red Army. Once more, information reached Moscow via 'Lucy' that uncovered the German's bluff. In the gallery of portraits of the 'Glorious Heroes who saved the Soviet Union' fighting Paulus at Stalingrad, the largest frame should have been reserved for the German émigré in Lucerne.

Rokossovski sent an ultimatum to Paulus, who rejected it, believing perhaps in the last chance that was supposed to be coming from Kharkov. As at the beginning of this campaign of 1942, Russian loud-speakers revealed the truth to the Wehrmacht, robbing the troops of their last illusions. Then, knowing that they would meet with little resistance, seven Soviet armies, sixty shock divisions, went quickly to work. To make matters worse for the Germans, the cold, the eternal ally of the Russians, was also present at the battle. Very little German blood flowed that day: it froze in the bodies of the dead.

On December 25, 1942, General Guisan celebrated Christmas with the 2nd Light Infantry Regiment on the public square at Aarberg. He knew no more than the rest of his compatriots of the plans Walter Schellenberg was presenting to Heinrich Himmler for approval.

Schellenberg could not have failed to notice the change that had come over his superior in the past months. His shoulders seemed to droop even more than before and his eyes, hidden behind thick lenses, seemed more globular than ever. His upper lip twitched intermittently. The SS-Reichsführer played nervously with the famous green pencil he used to annotate all the reports that passed through his podgy fingers—and with which he so often signed orders for the extermination of Jews.

"Are you sure the plan will be a success, Schellenberg?"

"I'll take responsibility for it."

"And you're sure Canaris, Beck and their gang are not behind it?"

"I'm convinced of it, Reichsführer. We can go on playing with them."

Himmler did not conceal his satisfaction with Schellenberg's plan. The trick his subordinate intended to play on the Swiss was very much to his taste. The encouragement he had given this young man had, he felt, been amply justified. He had proved an apt successor to Reinhard Heydrich.

A week later, Himmler entered the Führer's office in his headquarters. Goering, Goebbels, Rosenberg and Bormann, whom he detested, were all there. He explained that he would like the OKW to work out as soon as possible a plan to invade Switzerland. He knew that the generals would oppose such an enterprise, but they never did have any political sense.

Hitler observed the head of the SS attentively. What, he must have wondered, lay behind this latest plan of Himmler's. Was it part of some vast scheme directed against his personal enemies? Why Switzerland? The 6th Army was dying in Russia and it was even possible that the whole Wehrmacht in the East would collapse. Hitler had too much on his mind to concern himself with a pigmy like Switzerland, However, Himmler must have his reasons for wanting this and the Führer gave the desired approval.

The next morning, the order arrived at Zossen, the permanent headquarters of the Oberkommando of the Wehrmacht. For a fortnight nothing was done about the order. Then, when an order from the Führer himself arrived, the commissions set to work.

On Saturday, January 30, at 9 a.m., Rudolf Roessler arrived at the Villa Stutz. He seemed preoccupied, even troubled. The night before *Werther* had informed him that the OKW was preparing plans for an invasion of Switzerland under General Dietl. This was certainly a bombshell for Masson and Guisan. Yet, curiously enough, Roessler felt no more than a sense of unease. There was something suspicious about this information. It did not fit in with what he thought must be the concerns of the Nazi leaders at that time. He confided his doubts to Christian Schneider, his 'cut-out'.

A thousand kilometres away in Berlin, Walter Schellenberg waited anxiously for the results of his plan. He had alerted all his spies in the Confederation. They were to observe particularly closely all Swiss troop movements. At the slightest sign of any unusual activity on the other side of the Rhine, he would have his proof that one or several spies were to be found within the OKW, and that they were passing information to the Swiss, who on occasion informed the Allies.

16

SCHELLENBERG EXPECTED THE
Swiss to lie low, at least for a time. But if they were really
involved in this extraordinary affair they would come out
of hiding soon enough.

At the beginning of 1943, the SS-Brigadeführer thought
he fully understood the way the Swiss reacted to situations,
and he supplemented his own opinions with the reports of
his agents. Switzerland, he had decided, was a timorous
country, so lacking in resolution that whenever it thought
fit to concede something to one side it always felt obliged
to follow it at once by a concession to the other side.

The francophilia of General Guisan, for example, was
balanced by M. Pilar-Golaz, the head of the Political
Department. Pilar-Golaz had given public receptions for
such notorious National-Socialists as the German writer,
Jacob Schaffner, who had wanted to form a Nazi movement
in Switzerland. He had also given the German legation the
unusual privilege of having a direct telephone line with its
government in Berlin.

It was true that certain Swiss industrialists were unwilling to deliver arms to the Wehrmacht. But the Swiss banks, preserving their customary discretion, placed their numbered safes at the disposal of anonymous customers, which was extremely useful when one wanted to hide plundered wealth.

Switzerland also showed an irritating tolerance towards British and French spies and a no less marked hostility towards German secret agents. But it allowed the Reich 300 million Swiss francs per year, as trade between the two countries slightly favoured the Confederation, which was something of a consolation.

Finally, Colonel Victor Henry, the Swiss Commissioner for Internment, rendered innumerable services to members of the French resistance, while the Federal Council showed itself to be intransigent towards the Jews who asked for asylum.

It was this absence of concession to distress—a complete contradiction of Switzerland's professed humanitarian vocation—that convinced Schellenberg that, ever since 1939, the Confederation had been taking a dangerous risk. For the SS-Brigadeführer did not hesitate to connect these two problems: the treason affair with which he was mainly concerned, and the conduct of the Swiss state towards refugees, which gave the impression that even in this matter the Swiss wished to practise their usual balancing act.

We shall strictly refrain from following the SS general step by step in the talks he had in 1945 with the British secret service. But it is obvious that his interpretation throws startling light on one of the most disturbing episodes in Switzerland's conduct during the war:

"In exchange for their participation in your victory, the Swiss, or at least some of the Swiss leaders, sacrificed thousands of human lives to Hitler's madness. Not, of course, Swiss lives, but those of the desperate men and women who came and asked for asylum—Jews. Perhaps 100,000 . . . They were turned away, thrown back into the hands of my countrymen, who sent them off to concentration camps."

Coming from an SS-Brigadeführer, these words are somewhat surprising. But it must not be forgotten that in 1945 Schellenberg, too, tried to buy his life, in exchange for his disclosures to the British. Schellenberg's statements have been checked against an official document, written in 1953 at the request of the Federal Council by Carl Ludwig, a professor from Basle. It was a private report intended only for the Swiss deputies, but some of them, moved by the protests and even threats to cause a public scandal coming from Jewish international organisations, brought the affair out into the open.

It was only on October 10, 1942, that Walter Schellenberg learnt of the extent of the measures taken by the Swiss against the refugees. He was astonished to hear that the day before General Guisan had ordered the 1st and 4th Army Corps to reinforce the frontiers in the sectors of Geneva and the Bas-Valais. In fact, on October 10, the 1st Army Corps began sealing these zones off with barbed wire and forming a no-man's land between Switzerland and France.

"An operation intended only to prevent the Jews from entering the country," the Bureau 'F' in Berne explained to the SS-Brigadeführer.

"Open a dossier on the problem," Schellenberg replied.

The inquiry, conducted by German secret agents in Switzerland, went back to 1939, to the first day of the war.

From criteria based on the fear of famine and on the fear of contagious diseases that might be brought into the country by foreigners, on the uncertainty of the future in short, the Confederation had long calculated that the twenty-five cantons of the country would certainly not be able to support more than 7,000 aliens. As 7,100 refugees had already been granted asylum since 1933, the problem was quite clear. Even before the thousands of unfortunates began beating on its walls, Switzerland had declared that it had reached its limit and was unable to take more.

For those aliens living in its territory, Switzerland had drawn up strict obligations. They were forbidden to indulge in political activities or do anything that might imperil the nation's neutrality. They were forbidden to earn money without the prior consent of the police. They were forbidden to leave the residence assigned to them. They were forbidden to enter, let alone stay, in any hotel or boarding-house. Their aliens' card would bear an unmistakable stamp. And when any of these aliens came into the slightest contact with Swiss citizens, they must 'announce themselves', that is to say, they must say immediately that they were aliens.

These obligations were complemented by a regulation which stated that the cantons would return to the country from which they had come, without formalities, all foreigners who had illegally entered the country since the beginning of the war. This regulation did not apply either to deserters or political refugees. But this last description, which was used to cover resisters, was never applied to the Jews.

However, at the beginning of September 1939, Switzerland opened her doors to two fugitives. They took up residence at the Lausanne-Palace hotel, announced that their large entourage would be following shortly and that they would all be staying 'for some time'. The two residents were the Maharajah of Kapurthala and his son, Amarjip Singh. These were no ordinary aliens and, indeed, Switzerland showed a similar tolerance towards a few thousand other rich foreigners. They were merely asked to contribute, according to their means, to the private institutions that had been set up to give help to refugees. But it was understood, of course, that these privileged foreigners should in no way be a danger to the security of the Confederation.

The same tolerance was not extended to fugitives, however famous they may have been, who were recognised as enemies of Nazism—as in the case of Professor Foerster, for example.

Walter Schellenberg had not forgotten this affair. On March 13, 1936, the SD had forced this eminent German philosopher to leave the Reich on account of his pacifist tendencies and his hostile attitude towards the régime.

In September 1939, Wilhelm Foerster applied to

Switzerland from Paris for a special visa, for himself and his family. Berne refused, allowing him only to give a few lectures, if the war made it possible. So in May 1940, the professor was in Geneva when the Wehrmacht invaded France. On June 22, he asked permission to stay until the Locarno-Barcelona air-line was re-opened, when he would go to Portugal. The aliens section of the police refused and Foerster and his family were extradited on July 10, 1940—though to unoccupied France, it is true.

Aliens were no more fortunate if they happened to be Jews. Jeannet W was a German Jewess from Freiburg-am-Brisgau. In autumn 1941, she got a lawyer in Basle to apply for a visa to Switzerland, or any other country, for herself and her daughter, who was not Jewish. The lawyer obtained safe-conducts to Cuba and booked two tickets for a ship that was leaving in December. All he now needed was transit visas from Switzerland so that his clients could go through non-occupied France into Portugal. Berne refused —and Jeanette W and her daughter ended their lives in a gas-chamber.

It was not with indignation—he would have tended rather to approve—but with curiosity that Schellenberg wondered how Switzerland had managed to accept no more than three hundred and eight refugees, almost entirely Jews, between September 1939 and January 1942. He was not counting General Prugar's ten thousand five hundred Polish soldiers, fighting with the French 45th Army Corps, who had entered Switzerland on June 19, 1940, and been stationed in the region of Lyss-Büreau. The Confederation itself regarded them as military internees—and, as such, they came under different regulations.

Switzerland had shown mercy to these three hundred and eight refugees—mainly German and Dutch Jews—as a sop to the consciences of a number of national councillors, including Maag and Rittmeyer, who had begun to voice their disquiet. At the instigation of these councillors, who had expressed their concern to help them to overcome the deterioration in their morale, the refugees were to be put into camps where they could work for the Swiss Army.

The engineer Otto Zaugg was put in charge of the organisation that was set up for the purpose. The first camp was opened on April 9, 1940, at Felsberg. Others followed. There were finally thirty-seven in all—as well as fourteen quarantine camps, twenty-one reception camps, thirty-one homes and eight selection camps. The refugees were given free transport from the residence camps to the work camps. They received a wage of 1 Swiss franc per day. They were lent overalls and shoes.

Tens of thousands of unfortunates aspired to these barbed-wired paradises—even to the camp at Cropettes, near Geneva, where there was one water-tap per ten people, and where the inmates slept on straw that was changed every three weeks; or to the camp at Champeix, where the food was so poor and so inadequate that the camp was nick-named 'World's End'; or to the camp at Büren, where the work consisted of digging peat in difficult conditions. But they were unable to get there. Instead, they were sent to other camps, in Germany, where they met with a far more terrible fate.

From January 1942, in fact, the numbers of Jews who appeared every day at the Swiss frontier and who were sent back, after being caught trying to crowd their way through the police posts, increased considerably. Between January and April 1942, eighty-two had succeeded in being admitted. At the end of July there were eight hundred and fifty in all, of whom three hundred and thirty-five were Dutch.

Then came the massive deportations organised by the Germans throughout Europe. The danger became acute for all Jews. They rushed towards Switzerland but were turned back. There were protests, of course. But the officials responsible for refugees would not listen. The refugees were sorted according to nationality. The women were separated from the men and the Jews from the Catholics, Protestants and non-religious. For them it was a financial and organisational problem. A work camp was viable only if it had at least sixty internees. Moreover, it cost money to set up such a centre. Cement, pipes and electric wire had to be obtained and laid.

Two methods were used by the Swiss to expel the unwanted refugees. They were smuggled back across the frontier. They had a nine out of ten chance of being recaptured on the other side of course. But at least they had some chance of survival. This method was possible only in the Jura and Grisons mountains. The second method was nothing less than a simple condemnation. The refugee was handed over to the police of the country from which he had come. This method, which was more generally used than the other, had one serious disadvantage for the Swiss: it gave rise to some very embarrassing scenes.

To escape this terrible fate, Schellenberg revealed to the British Secret service, many refugees preferred to kill themselves at the frontiers. Professor Ludwig, the author of the federal report on the Swiss policy towards refugees, confirms this revelation. A brief accusatory note on p. 239 of his report reads:

"They often committed suicide at the feet of the Swiss soldiers in order not to fall into the hands of the Germans."

It was not this dramatic fact, but the sharp increase in the numbers of refugees at the Swiss frontiers, since July 30, 1942, that alarmed Herr Rothmund, the head of the Federal police. Jews were still getting through from the French side of the Jura mountains. He asked for motorised formations to patrol the frontiers. The Federal Council granted his request.

On August 4, 1942, he ordered that the rejection of refugees should continue to be observed strictly, "even if it results in serious risks for these persons, that is, injury or death," he added. He recalled that only deserters and political refugees should be admitted—denying once again that this description fitted the Jews. On September 26, 1942, he maintained this discrimination in a new decree, declaring —in the face of all the information that reached him—that the Jews were in no serious danger in Europe at that time!

Swiss Jewish organisations protested. They alerted the

Red Cross and the Swiss centre for aid to refugees. On August 13, 1942, Saly B, president of the Swiss federation of Jewish communities, invited Herr Rothmund to a meeting with the central committee of the federation. He was told about concentration camps and Nazi atrocities running into thousands of deaths. He dismissed their pleas with these words:

"We must be content to look after the Jews we have already saved. In any case, German officials have assured me that the detainees in these camps are only made to work. They are not harshly treated. There can be no question of rescinding our decrees. Switzerland will remain closed to the Jews."

The agitation reached the Federal Council. Herr Rothmund had been taken to task by many people. Councillor Oeri predicted a serious internal crisis if the decisions of the Council were retained. The Socialist Party and the Federation of Protestant churches began to agitate against the decisions.

This mounting opposition began to have its effect. On August 23, 1942, M. de Steiger ordered the frontiers to be opened for pregnant women, young children and the very old. But fourteen days later, at a meeting of the cantonal police chiefs at Altdorf, Herr Rothmund terrified the authorities by revealing that since July, in less than a month, a thousand new refugees had been arrested for entering the country illegally. Their cases would be examined before any decision was taken as to whether they should be extradited or not. The Federal Council was not alone in the intransigence of its attitude. The vast majority of the cantons themselves were just as severe towards the refugees. It was they, on September 10, 1942, who demanded a tightening up of frontier controls.

The canton of the City of Basle was the only exception. Although it had to take in a great many refugees before the war, it declared that it was willing to take in more. It was Basle that received most of the refugees' children—Saint-Gall and Tessin being also among the more hospitable.

When the humane attitude of Basle became known, other cantons did not hesitate to get rid of their own refugees by leaving them in the market place of that city.

Other cantons acted more cynically. They warned those refugees that they wished to get rid of that if they were found on the territory of the canton after nightfall, they would be sent into Germany that night. In this way, the canton saved the price of transport. The refugees, who had also heard of the generosity of Basle, had no alternative but to try and seek refuge there.

Some cantons refused to accept any refugees who could not support themselves. They tolerated only a few rich individuals whom they held, literally, to ransom. Others were so violently hostile to the refugees that they even refused them permission to cross their territory on their way to other places that had accepted them.

Herr Rothmund had no difficulty, therefore, following an oral report before the Federal Council on September 22, 1942, in getting the Confederation to strengthen its frontiers.

"Since the beginning of the war," he declared, "two thousand five hundred refugees have entered our country illegally. When these are added to the seven thousand one hundred refugees who have been in residence here since 1933, we get a total of nine thousand six hundred. Need I remind you that our experts have calculated that we cannot support more than seven thousand. Since the beginning of the war the upkeep of these foreigners has cost seventeen million francs—of this, five million have been paid by the Confederation itself and the rest by private institutions. This situation must not be allowed to continue. There are no longer enough frontier guards to stop the flow of fugitives; they must be backed up by military police and if that is not enough, we shall have to call in the army itself."

The Radical Democratic group approved Herr Rothmund's proposals. The Peasants-Artisans-Bourgeois expressed their satisfaction. The Catholic Conservatives also agreed. The Social Democrats, the Liberal Democrats and the Independents made no comment. Only a handful of councillors protested: Graber, Maag, Rittmeyer, Oeri. Thus, on October 9, 1942, the Federal Council asked General Guisan to take over responsibility for the frontiers—and Walter Schellenberg was duly informed by his agents.

From this point Schellenberg never ceased to observe the behaviour of the Swiss towards the refugees. Like the Swiss authorities, he kept an account of the situation. In the 'debit' column he wrote the number of refugees accepted by Switzerland; in the 'credit' column those it had turned away and who had been caught by his SS colleagues. The Federal authorities simply changed the headings of the two columns, placing to its 'credit' those it had saved from the Nazis. But otherwise both sets of figures agree substantially.

Between September 1939 and October 1942, four thousand seven hundred refugees had been granted asylum by the Confederation. On December 31, 1942, there were nine thousand one hundred. At the end of the war, adding together these civilian refugees, the military internees and the German and Allied deserters, Switzerland reached a total of one hundred thousand. These were approximately the same number of refugees turned away at the frontiers and picked up by the SS.

It is now easier to understand why Walter Schellenberg linked the enormous espionage affair that obsessed him and the strange intransigence of the Swiss authorities towards the Jews. It was, in a sense, something that the Swiss could throw into the scales as a counter-balance should the Germans ever discover the role they had been playing with the Allies.

Another fact confirmed Walter Schellenberg in his hypothesis: the no less surprising silence of the Swiss authorities concerning the delicate problem of their knowledge of the atrocities inflicted by the Nazis on Jews and non-Jews alike in the concentration camps.

Paradoxical as it may seem, until 1944, when the fate of Germany had been finally sealed, the Swiss appeared to know nothing of the genocide being practised by the Nazis.

In October 1942, Herr Rothmund visited the concentration camp at Oranienburg. It was with "a certain curiosity" —the words are his own—that Schellenberg awaited the reactions of the head of the Federal Police. He was not disappointed. In a statement to the Federal Council, Herr Rothmund said simply:

"I must admit that the Jews are not treated with much consideration in this camp. But nothing led me to believe that they were being executed *en masse* there."

However, since March 16, 1942—seven months—Switzerland had officially known that the Germans organised mass executions in their concentration camps.

That day, Dr Rudolf B of Zurich, was called to the Federal palace in Berne by the public prosecutor of the army, Brigadier Eugster, and by Herr Kobelt, head of the Military Department. Rudolf B had just taken part in a medical mission and tour in the countries of eastern Europe. In January 1942, he had been taken into the confidence of a German medical officer, Captain Wagner, attached to the quarantine camp north of Smolensk.

"In the camps," said Wagner, "the massacre of Jews is increasing. Gas chambers and crematoria are functioning at full capacity. With my own eyes, I've seen women digging their own graves, and SS murdering children and old people with bullets in the back of their necks. A woman told me about the early days in Auschwitz. A lot of blood, a lot of suffering, a lot of deaths. . ."

This categorical, accusatory account disturbed Eugster and Kobelt. They refused to take notes of the conversation that had taken place. They ordered Dr Rudolf B to remain silent and never repeat what he had just said.

Rudolf B did not keep silent. He talked. He even entrusted to Professor Carl Ludwig, the author of the report on Swiss policy towards the refugees, the diary of one of his friends, Sergeant W, who had accompanied him on the mission to eastern Europe.

Rudolf B had also shown it to the Public Prosecutor of the army—and Brigadier Eugster had sent it back to him with an accompanying letter which showed he had read it and that he was now aware of the abundant notes W had taken concerning the extermination taking place in the German camps. In May 1944 Dr B repeated his declarations in public and Kobelt and Eugster reproached him with having violated professional secrecy.

The Swiss knew. There were other informers. A Swiss citizen living privately in the Ukraine also witnessed mass executions of Jews at the beginning of August 1942, at Kamen-Kasirski, in the Rokitno marshes. This witness was in constant touch with the Swiss Consul in Hamburg and sent him detailed information. This information was then conveyed to Berne. At about the same time a Bavarian civil servant living in Berlin, told a senior civil servant at the Swiss legation of measures being taken to exterminate Jews. Information from these and other sources found its way to the office of Dr G M Riegner, director of the office of the World Jewish Congress in Geneva.

So it was in vain that the Federal authorities muzzled even their newspapers, such as the *Volkstimme*, which wanted to disclose the truth about the massacre of seventy thousand Jews at Kiev.

Walter Schellenberg was not to be hoodwinked for long: if the Swiss were silencing their consciences and refusing to acknowledge what they knew, it was because they were too fully committed to the Allied cause elsewhere. The trap that he had set, with the support of Heinrich Himmler, would soon give him the full answer.

17

FROM THE MIDDLE OF JANUARY
to Wednesday, March 3, 1943, Walter Schellenberg lived
on his nerves. He had been waiting for proof that the
Confederation was directly linked to an informer within
the Oberkommando of the Wehrmacht. Fear that his trap
had not worked was beginning to grip him when, that
Wednesday evening, the tension slackened. At Biglen, in
Switzerland, at the end of the interview he had requested
with General Guisan, Brigadier Masson had at last decided
to put his head in the noose held out to him. Schellenberg's
pleasure in his victory soon began to pall, however: it was
one thing to *know*, quite another to act on one's knowledge.

There was no witness to what passed between the two
secret service chiefs when they met on March 12, in Zürich.
Nevertheless, there is no reason to doubt the version given
to the British after the war by Walter Schellenberg, and
two facts show without the slightest doubt that the relaxed
atmosphere Schellenberg had tried to promote in relations
between the Reich and Switzerland had disappeared.

The SS-Brigadeführer was deeply apprehensive about the

meeting in Zürich on March 12. He feared that Masson, realising retrospectively that he had made a serious blunder a few days previously at Biglen, might have him arrested or even executed. Schellenberg would have done as much in Masson's position. So he took the greatest possible precautions. He arranged to be followed by a host of agents supplied from the espionage centres of the Sicherheits- dienst in Switzerland. They escorted him at a distance, with their fingers on the triggers of their guns, throughout his walk with Masson along the left bank of the Limmat. At the first sign of violence from the Swiss, Masson would no doubt have been killed on the spot.

A second fact that emerged was the change of tactics adopted by Schellenberg. On the surface nothing had changed. On March 23, eleven days after the Zürich meet- ing, Masson told Bernard Barbey, so that General Guisan would know of it, that the OKW had dropped their plans to invade Switzerland and that he had learnt this through his extremely 'valuable' contact, Walter Schellenberg. The amicable relations seemed as strong as ever. In fact, things were very different.

This time Schellenberg did not dupe Masson. For Masson realised that what Schellenberg had been unable to get by charm he now wanted by force. And if Masson had not taken certain precautions, the SS-Brigadeführer might well have got his hands on Rudolf Roessler, and probably on *Werther* and *Olga* as well. Perhaps, too, the OKW would have revived their plans to invade the Confederation.

On Schellenberg's orders, almost every German agent in Switzerland was brought into the chase. Their mission was to concentrate their attention on Geneva and Lausanne, which, Schellenberg now knew, were the key cities. He intended reaching his objective by the only weak spot he knew: its radio communications.

For more than a month, goniometry had been used simultaneously from the German, Italian and French frontiers. It was discovered that at least one transmitter sent occasional dispatches to Moscow from Geneva, while at

Lausanne another, probably the main transmitter, sent out long, regular broadcasts.

The German spies were not left to their own devices. They had a plan: a systematic attempt to penetrate a precisely defined area. The idea was Schellenberg's. He knew the Swiss and their congenital prudence. He did not imagine that their secret service, whatever its convictions, would officially communicate information to the western Allies, let alone the Russians. Although he could not see exactly how they sent their information to London, on the other hand he felt sure he knew how it was sent to Moscow. The work was almost certainly done by Swiss communists. Moreover, since Stalingrad, they had many sympathisers among the socialists. It was on these Left-wing circles that his spies were to concentrate their attention.

There was no flaw in Schellenberg's reasoning. It proved, if proof was needed, that there was little he did not know about his Swiss neighbours. In the Swiss elections on October 31, 1943, there was, for the first time, a marked improvement in the performance of the socialists. They gained nine seats in the National Council and five in the Council of the States. This was undeniably the result of Russian military successes.

The BUPO, or Swiss counter-espionage service, did not at first lose its self-possession over this new wave of German espionage activity. As the cafés, clubs and cinemas frequented by the Left-wing citizens of Geneva and Lausanne became inundated with these outsiders, the Swiss riposted by arresting one after another of the leading German spies in the Confederation.

Rudolf Roessler also noticed a change in the atmosphere. The shadowy figures whose job it was to protect him became ever more numerous. He could no longer be unaware of them as he travelled between Wesemlin and the Vita Nova Verlag or visited the Villa Stutz at Kastanienbaum. However, he continued with his work, as seemingly imperturbable as ever. In the East, the Russians had embarked on a series of victories; it was not the time for 'Lucy' to sit back

193

and take a rest. Moscow constantly asked for information.

April, May and June, which in the previous year had been marked by intensive military preparation—the positioning of the springboards necessary for the offensives—were calm in 1943. The Wehrmacht was binding its wounds. Opposite, the Red Army waited. This strategic method was to serve it well in the last six months of the year. The 'wearing-down' tactics it had so far used had been sufficiently profitable not to be exchanged for others, at least not yet. Moreover, the Russians knew that the Wehrmacht was preparing to launch a new attack.

'Lucy' had kept the Kremlin up to date on the plans of the OKW. New heavy tanks, 'Tigers', had been sent to the front. There were enough of them to equip seventeen panzer divisions. The Führer was depending on them. 500,000 men would be thrown into the battle—'the flower of the German Army', as William L. Shirer called them in *The Third Reich*. Field Marshal Guenther Hans von Kluge had himself worked out the overall plan of what was to become the second large-scale German defeat in Russia— the offensive that Hitler had named 'Operation Citadel'.

It was planned to encircle—still the same tactics—a million Russian troops forming a huge salient in the Wehrmacht lines west of Kursk, a town situated at the confluence of the Tuskor and the Kura, the great Georgian river. Kursk was an important railway junction, an industrial centre planted in the heart of a district of orchards, grain-fields and grazing land.

Von Kluge had three armies spread out over a distance of 120 kilometres, between Kharkov and Orel. The 9th, seven of whose twenty divisions were armoured, was to operate from the south to the north. The 4th, comprising seventeen divisions, plus an SS armoured division, was to attack from Kharkov, from the north to the south. Lastly, the 2nd Army—six armoured divisions and two infantry divisions— were to face the Russians head on. A classic pincer movement, which, if the enemy was not expecting it, could prove one of the major victories of the campaign.

But unfortunately for von Kluge and the Reich, the enemy knew all about it, down to the last details. Rudolf Roessler had sent them abundant information in his dispatches. Once again, *Werther* had brought off a masterpiece of military intelligence. Everything was there: the sectors to be attacked, the numbers of men and material that would be used, the positions of the supply posts and of the command posts, the proximity of possible reinforcements, 'D' day and 'H' hour.

On July 5, 1943, there were large-scale infantry preparations on the German front. Von Kluge's troops moved into the attack, and then came the shattering reply. The Russians had filled their salient with guns and tanks.

On July 10, as the western Allies were landing in Sicily, and the Swiss were considering a general mobilisation in case of a sudden advance in Italy, the Wehrmacht gained about ten kilometres at Kursk. The Russians had let all the famous heavy 'Tiger' tanks enter the net, where they were to be blown up. The Russians had full details of the capability of these tanks and had been able to put in the right guns to meet them. On July 22, seventeen days after the beginning of the offensive, the Germans had no more tanks. The Wehrmacht retreated, thoroughly defeated.

Sure of their own forces and knowing, through Roessler, the state of German troops along the rest of the front, the Russians did not wait for the end of the massacre at Kursk to launch an attack themselves—on the German salient at Orel. From the middle of July 1943 to the taking of Berlin in 1945, they never lost the initiative.

On August 4, 1943, the Red Army drove the Wehrmacht out of Orel. The next day, Bielgorod was taken. On August 23, Kharkov. At Kursk everything had long been over. On September 20, Briansk was recaptured. Smolensk followed on the 25th. Then the whole industrial basin of the Donetz. Then the Dnieper. On November 6, Kiev fell to the Russians. By the end of this fatal year for the Reich, the Russian armies in the south broke through the frontiers of

Rumania and Poland and had practically completed the liberation of their own country.

In Switzerland a battle of another kind had broken out between General Guisan and the authorities. Sensing a possible danger in the first Allied landings on Italian territory—namely, a 'preventative occupation' of Switzerland by Germany alone—the head of the Swiss Army considered it reasonable to make plans for a possible general mobilisation. However, M. Pilet-Golaz, the head of the Political Department, refused—wishing, above all, not to invoke the displeasure of the Germans.

It was also at this time that the new tactics adopted by Schellenberg in his dealings with Switzerland began to pay off. At Geneva, his agents had set up a provisional base near the Gare de Cornavin, in a hotel run by a Swiss Nazi, and had completed lists of Left-wing suspects and were now building up information about their activities. There was one name on the Geneva list that, had he known, would have given Alexander Rado a bad moment—that of Margareta Bolli.

In Lausanne, the Nazis had been even more successful. They had succeeded in placing two double agents in Rado's network—again on Schellenberg's initiative. In order to be absolutely sure of success, Schellenberg had even thought of using the best Soviet agents who had been captured by the Sicherheitsdienst throughout Europe, and who had agreed to work for the Germans in exchange for life and security.

This was how Georg and Johanna Wilmer, known in the espionage world as 'Lorenz' and 'Laura', turned up in Switzerland at this time. These highly experienced spies were well known to the 'Centre', which had been using them since 1926. They had lived and worked for a long time in Japan, which they left in 1935. They spent a brief training period at the Soviet spy school at Sekhjodnya, just outside Moscow. It was there that they met another student, Alexander Rado, with whom they became friends. When, in 1936, the MGB decided to send three hundred of its best agents into and around Germany, the Wilmers were among them, for they were both gifted photographers and micro-photographers.

When war broke out in Europe in 1939, the 'Centre' lost all trace of 'Lorenz' and 'Laura'. They had been caught by the Sicherheitsdienst and sent to the Ploetzensee, the huge prison in Berlin where the members of the 'July 20' plot were later to be hanged. The Wilmers knew that the Germans were always willing to use specialists—so they were saved by their ability to reduce a message the size of a normal sheet of paper to the size if a full-stop at the end of a sentence.

Schellenberg soon discovered Georg Wilmer's Achilles' heel. This man liked money—in fact, he had lost his communist faith largely because of this. It was an easy matter to take Johanna with him. So for a long time they worked in the archives of the Sicherheitsdienst, helping the Germans capture a large number of their former colleagues. When the German spies in Geneva told Schellenberg they had drawn up an interesting list of suspects belonging to or close to Léon Nicole's Swiss Communist Party, the SS-Brigade-führer called on the services of the Wilmers.

He allowed the couple to roam freely around Geneva. Within a fortnight they had met Rado. The reunion appeared to be an amicable one, but actually Alexander Rado had found their explanations somewhat unconvincing. They claimed they had escaped from Germany shortly after the beginning of the war and had taken refuge in German-speaking Switzerland, where they had done everything possible to remain unnoticed. Then, wishing to take up espionage work once more and to help the 'Centre' in its fight against Nazism—for they still had valuable contacts in Germany—they had decided to frequent the activities of the Swiss Communist Party in the hope of meeting up with former colleagues. Could Rado inform the MGB that they were once more available?

The resident-director's first decision was to double the precautions he took to preserve the secret of where he lived.

He even went so far as to rent a luxury flat in Berne where he sent his wife, Helene, and their two sons. For he, like Roessler and Masson, had noticed there was a lot going on in Switzerland at that time, especially in Geneva.

His second decision was typical of his egotism. He had somewhat resented the independence accorded by the 'Centre' to Alexander Foote. This Englishman, who should really be working as a wireless-operator, under his direction, had been promoted—owing no doubt to the value of the information communicated to him by 'Lucy'. The MGB, he felt, had almost got to the point of regarding Foote as the equal of himself, the resident-director. He was still suspicious of the Wilmers—so he decided to send them to Foote. If anything went wrong, then it would rebound on him.

When Rado next met the couple he advised them to go to Lausanne and get in touch with him again when they had found lodgings. He would then introduce them to one of the most important members of his network. This comrade communicated regularly with the 'Centre' and would be able to use them. In any case, they were not to come back to Geneva: he did not feel very safe there at the moment and did not wish to put them in danger too.

Georg and Johanna Wilmer went to Lausanne, where they rented a luxurious villa overlooking the city. The ostentation with which they spent Schellenberg's money quickly won them the respect of their neighbours. The time had now come for them to meet their new masters. Their lines were cast. It would not be long before the big fish began to bite.

This surpassed all Schellenberg's hopes. Until then nothing had led him to suppose that the Russians operated a network in Switzerland—and what a network! How could it have escaped for so long the permanent investigations of his agents? He would not now be surprised to learn that the Swiss used this channel to communicate their information to Moscow. For he knew Masson too well to imagine for a single moment that he did not know of the existence of this network.

Switzerland did not cease to astonish him. This so very bourgeois nation, that regarded communism as the scourge of God, that had even sent doctors to the eastern front to give medical attention to German troops in the name of the crusade against Bolshevism, this same nation was capable, at the same time, of helping the Soviet Union, in the worst possible way, through espionage.

Schellenberg considered that he had been given a good lesson in double-facedness. He must now do everything possible to make up for the time lost. First, he must leave the Wilmers to strike their big fish, as they said, and also wait for his agents in Geneva to do their work. Then they would all be caught at once. He knew how to make people talk.

18

ALEXANDER FOOTE DID NOT
hide his dislike of the Wilmers. Georg struck him as being
altogether too fluent, too vain, too self-satisfied. Johanna,
on the other hand, seemed too silent and withdrawn; her
eyes had a hunted look about them. And how were they
able to rent such a magnificent house? How did they get
permission when the law concerning the residence of
foreigners in Switzerland was so strict? Where did they
get the money which they spent so freely? Although he
waxed so eloquent about his pre-war days, this 'Lorenz'
kept strangely silent about his activities since 1939. No,
Foote neither liked nor trusted Georg and Johanna Wilmer.

Anxious to receive Foote in a manner fitting the
importance Rado had attributed to him, the Wilmers did
not spare any expense—excellent food and wine, followed
by the best cigars. Johanna took little part in the conversation, but watched attentively over their guest's needs, never
allowing his glass to remain anything but full. Over coffee,
Wilmer talked at length and in the most emphatic way of
the importance of the contacts he had preserved. They

continued to supply him regularly with information—from France, where he had friends in the Maquis and even in Germany, where he knew valuable anti-Nazis. It would be a pity, he added, not to put such information to use.

After these obviously pressing offers of collaboration came a flood of questions—on Foote's activities, on how often he was in radio contact with the 'Centre', on his changes of codes and wavelengths. Wilmer's manner was that of a friend 'talking shop', but Foote sensed beneath the cameraderie a formidable and insidious technique of investigation.

Foote fended off the questions and followed Rado's example that night of making innumerable détours and doublings back to get home, 20 Chemin de Longeraie. No, he argued to himself, he did not like people who threw themselves at you and talked and talked—and tried to get you to talk. Rado, whom he consulted by telephone, was not reassuring and simply advised him to inform the 'Centre'—he did not need to be told that.

However, he had an unpleasant surprise. Moscow refused to share his doubts. The Wilmers were certainly good agents and had spent years in the service of the workers' cause, etc. Their way of life did not matter: it was a well-known habit of theirs which they had picked up in the course of frequenting the rich and powerful in the capitalist world. Foote could work with them without fear.

But Foote's feeling of unease was only increased by later visits to the Wilmers. One evening, on his way home—having evaded all questions as to his address—he realised that his mackintosh had been searched, probably during dinner. He was in the habit of leaving odd pieces of paper about everywhere—but never anything that had to do with his work. There had been some papers of this kind in his trench coat. They were gone.

Next time, it was his jacket which was gone through. Wilmer had insisted he should take it off in order to feel more comfortable in the heat of the room. Johanna then took it to a coat-hanger in the hall. She found nothing.

Foote had concealed his wallet in his underclothes. Later, he went over his jacket himself and saw that it had been searched. He had taken the precaution of sewing a fine thread across one of the inside pockets. The thread had been broken.

His hosts plied him continually with questions about his work, even though he had remarked that in doing so they were contravening the strict injunctions to secrecy imposed by the 'Centre' on members of the same network. Every time he left their house he made ever greater détours to get home.

Alexander Foote finally became certain that the Wilmers were agents who had gone over to the enemy. This happened after an incident that took place on a Sunday early in the autumn of 1943.

It was a warm sunny day. After lunch and coffee, his host took him out to the garden in front of the villa. They talked casually, with their backs turned to the front of the house. Wilmer put his arm round the Englishman's shoulder, as he told a story, and suddenly, Foote realised that Wilmer had slewed him round. He raised his head with simulated nonchalance—and noticed, out of the corner of his eye, a camera lens pointing at him from a window on the first floor.

Foote gave no indication of what he had seen. He invented an urgent meeting, that he had forgotten about, and said he must leave at once. Johanna Wilmer, who only a few moments before had been behind the camera, was too embarrassed to look at Foote. Georg Wilmer, on the other hand, studied his face carefully, as if trying to make up his mind whether he should suddenly change his attitude. Foote did not give him time, but pushed past him and ran away as fast as he could.

That evening he told the 'Centre' that whatever orders they might give him he would not see the Wilmers again, being convinced that they were working for the Germans. Their reply came back the following night: "If you have convincing proof, break off relations. Move house."

As if a foreigner in war-time Switzerland, who was lucky

not to be interned, could move house just when he wished! Convinced that the Wilmers, or those they were working for, would try to turn Lausanne upside down to find him, Foote shut himself up in his flat, supplied with food by his charwoman. However, he was not to stay like that for long. Events were to come to a rapid head.

Brigadier Masson felt that Walter Schellenberg, or his agents, were beginning to get very hot in this game of hunt-the-slipper. He could not allow the fate of Switzerland to be exposed any longer to such danger. He was under no illusion. If, as he suspected, the Nazis soon reached their goal, if they got their hands on living proofs that the Soviet Union had agents in Switzerland, who worked there with impunity, not to say with the complicity of the Federal authorities, a major scandal would erupt. Moreover, if, by means of these living proofs, the Sicherheitsdienst reached Rudolf Roessler and thus implicated the Swiss secret service in a serious espionage affair against the Reich, nothing could save the country. One could not reasonably depend on the Swiss Army, however devoted it might be, to stop for long the advance of the Wehrmacht and SS.

There was only one thing to do: cut the ground from under the Germans' feet.

At 9 a.m. on October 8, 1943, two black cars filled with men in plain clothes, stopped in front of the tree-lined drive leading to 192 route de Florissant. The Hamels understood at once what was happening: the BUPO, or Swiss counterespionage, had arrived. While Edmond received the police, Olga ran upstairs and hung a duster out on a window-sill. Alexander Rado was expected—he came every day. A duster in the window was the alarm signal.

The BUPO had no difficulty in finding Hamel's transmitter—it was concealed in the basement among a mass of repairs. They then collected a pile of documents which would be sorted out and analysed later.

At just that moment, Alexander Rado arrived in the route de Florissant. He turned into the drive leading to the villa, when he noticed the two cars and the duster in the window.

Without showing the slightest surprise or curiosity, Rado turned back into the road. He walked on and then turned right into the long avenue Krieg, which curves northwards. He walked for five hundred metres, then turned left again, into the route de Malagnou. Another hundred metres and he took the first turning on the right, the rue Henri Mussard. Outwardly, the resident-director looked calm but inside he was panic-stricken. At the end of September, fearful for his own safety after the appearance of the Wilmers, he had taken all his papers to the Hamels. These included financial reports, copies of the messages for Moscow, codes of the transmissions and the list of agents with addresses. All this was now in the hands of the BUPO. However, he must try and save Margareta Bolli.

He arrived at 8 bis rue Mussard too late. The counter-espionage service had got there first. There were two cars there, but no alarm-signal. She obviously hadn't had the time. However, it wasn't necessary. Margareta Bolli emerged from the building flanked by two detectives, who led her to one of the cars. She did not look up. She had not seen him. Then, to Rado's stupefaction, two more guards appeared holding a handsome young man who was hand-cuffed. This arrogant, fair-haired athlete was called Hans Peters, a German spy working for the Sicherheitsdienst, and had been the young woman's lover for the past week. The BUPO had found them in bed. Yes, it really was time Brigadier Masson intervened, to save Rudolf Roessler, to save *Werther* and *Olga* and to save Switzerland.

Alexander Rado did not go back to his flat at 113 rue de Lausanne. He abandoned the Géo-Presse. He dropped everything and took the train for Berne where he joined his wife, Helene, and their two sons in his secret lodgings. On October 10, he telephoned Foote's flat from a public telephone box. He did not expect an answer. Foote, he felt sure, would already have been arrested.

"Hello? Foote?"

The Englishman recognised the voice at once. Rado only

telephoned him when something had gone wrong.

"Yes. What's the matter?"

"Edmond is very ill. The doctors decided he must be taken to hospital."

"Edmond?"

"Yes, Edmond! The day before yesterday. I want to see you. Come over to Berne. I'll meet you in the Botanical Gardens, near the Lorrainebrücke, the bridge near the station. Don't look for me, I'll find you."

Throughout the journey, Foote turned the matter over in his mind. He had understood perfectly that Hamel had been arrested. What would Rado decide to do? The resident-director must be dying of fear to give such a vague rendezvous. However, Rado found him easily enough. He seemed very nervous:

"Don't let's hang about. I'm sure the taxi-driver who drove me to the station recognised me. Just as I was walking away, I saw him look at a photograph and drive off at top speed. A Swiss technique. The police issue photographs of suspects to all the public services. I must disappear. I'm handing everything over to you."

"You don't think they'll arrest me."

"Warn the 'Centre'. For some reason I don't yet understand, the BUPO don't seem to suspect you yet. But they've got your name. It was in my papers, which were seized at Hamel's. Go on transmitting to the end. I have given your address and telephone number to all the survivors of the network, warning them to be vigilant. These include my two 'cut-outs' with 'Lucy', Christian Schneider and Rachel Duebendorfer. Good luck!"

October went by. November began. Each day, Rachel Duebendorfer, alias 'Sissi', or Christian Schneider, alias 'Taylor', passed the information on directly from 'Lucy' to Foote, now the head of the network. Otto Pünter, alias 'Pakbo' also gave him all the information collected by his group, 'Rot', in south Germany and which formerly had been transmitted by Hamel and Bolli. The 'Centre' confirmed Rado's decision and accepted Foote as its new resident-director, though anxiously wondering how much longer Foote would remain free.

Not much longer. The Sicherheitsdienst were getting very near his flat in the Chemin de Longeraie. Foote did not realise this, but Masson's service knew. They arrested two or three Germans but the next day others took over the search. When, these, too, were captured, they were immediately replaced. Foote remained Rudolf Roessler's last link with Moscow, which was why Masson was protecting him and leaving him free for as long as possible. But this immunity could not go on much longer.

Kiev had just been recaptured by the Russians. 'Lucy' contributed much to this victory—as he had done for Kursk, Kharkov, Orel and Smolensk. The Red Army's summer campaign seemed to have come to an end. Foote had sent the Kremlin the latest figures of the Wehrmacht's strength drawn up by the OKW. There remained 176 German divisions on the Russian front, grouped into eleven armies, three of which were armoured. Still fighting beside them were forty-five Rumanian, Hungarian and Finnish divisions. On the western front there were seventy-two divisions, eighteen in the Balkans, twenty-two in Italy, eleven in Norway and twelve in Germany. The Reich was obviously finished.

On November 18, 1943, Foote received the latest dispatches from Roessler-'Lucy' and he coded them for transmission. They concerned the newest German weapons: the new night fighters of the Luftwaffe, rocket-propelled for more rapid take-off and the 'Volksjäger', the first jet-propelled aircraft on which the German engineers were working furiously. Foote transmitted a large part of these documents to the 'Centre' the same night. He said he would send the rest the following night.

At 1.15 a.m. on November 20, 1943, Foote heard a stampede on the stairs, followed by a banging at his door. He thought of Wilmer and the Germans. He transmitted his last word, "Adieu" and broke off his dispatch.

The knocking on the door grew louder. He could not

escape, but he was determined to destroy everything. He poured some petrol into a large bowl, put in his codes and set light to them.

On the landing, his door was beginning to give. It wouldn't be easy—it was very strong. And when it had finally given, whoever was in such a hurry to find him would find another, equally strong, at the end of his hall.

The codes were destroyed by this time. He took a hammer and smashed the marvellous mechanism which had enabled him to correspond for so long, and so effectively with the 'Centre'—and which had enabled him to share, in his own way, the triumph of Stalingrad and the other victories of the summer of 1943, and the destruction of Nazism.

When the last obstacle separating him from his assailants had collapsed, Foote was calm. Only a pile of twisted metal remained of what had been a secret radio station. His calm turned to relief when he saw his 'aggressors'. It was not the Sicherheitsdienst, as he had feared, but Inspectors Pasche and Knecht of the BUPO, accompanied by Marc Pavot, their chief code-specialist.

There, too, they were only just in time. Among the projects in the SD archives was a plan to seize Foote, on November 23. It was to be done quite simply by sending in a number of agents after the charwoman, who had been in their pay for the past few days.

With these arrests made—arrests that were so vital to Switzerland—Brigadier Masson was able to relax. At the Bureau Ha, Rudolf Roessler was reassured as to the fate of his colleagues. However, he was now deprived of all means of communicating with Moscow and did not conceal his displeasure. The Russians would win easily now without his help; the Germans could not stop their advance. In any case, he could be more useful to the West, now that the war had started moving again.

The information that he carried every day to the Villa Stutz did not, unfortunately, receive the same welcome from the Western Allies as it had done from the Russians.

These innumerable reports must have found their way to some bureaucratic dead-end in London.

Yet Roessler took care in sorting out the information he received. To the British, he sent any details which concerned the 'V 1' and 'V 2' rockets. He continued to supply the Swiss with an ever increasing number of general analyses of the general war situation. Already he was beginning to sit back and wait serenely for the end of the war to come, having no idea what awaited him.

Schellenberg had not given up his search. His listening-station in Dresden had informed him that there were no more transmissions on the wavelengths they had been observing and which, until November, had been so frequently used. In stopping the transmissions to Moscow, Masson had pulled off a major trick. But Schellenberg had another card up his sleeve—or rather two, to be precise.

His agents had located Christian Schneider and Rachel Duebendorfer when they appeared at Foote's flat with 'Lucy's' messages. They continued to watch this couple closely and noticed that this man and woman sometimes met a Lucerne bookseller. A rapid inquiry revealed that the bookseller was a German émigré! Where did he spring from? Why had he not presented himself to the National-Socialist organisation set up by the party in Switzerland? Only one answer was possible: he was an enemy of the Reich. Perhaps he, too, was one of the gang passing information to the Russians. The search began again.

This time, Roger Masson decided to put an end to it once and for all. On May 9, 1944, Rudolf Roessler was escorted under heavy guard to Bois-Mermet, the prison of Lausanne. Christian Schneider, Rachel Duebendorfer, her daughter Tamara, and Paul Boetcher were taken to Sainte-Antoine, the Geneva prison.

A prison was about the only place in Switzerland which was inaccessible to the Sicherheitsdienst. Schellenberg knew this—as he also knew he had no other means left of fulfilling his mission. He had underestimated the little Swiss brigadier: Masson had beaten him hands down. He tried to stifle his intense bitterness over this failure by turning his full attention to an important event which was being planned 'secretly' in Berlin. The usual plotters intended to assassinate the Führer in the course of the summer— probably in July.

Roger Masson was now completely reassured. The Nazis could no longer get their hands on the least known, but the greatest and most effective secret agent of the Second World War. At the same time, he felt extraordinarily embarrassed.

In fact, by the end of May and the beginning of June 1944, the Swiss government was in a state of terror. German troops were massing in Alsace, accompanied by transport planes. It was said that about twenty divisions had been observed within an area of 200 kilometres around the Swiss frontier. Herr Jaeger, the Swiss minister in Hungary, reported a rumour that had been circulating in Budapest: Switzerland was about to be invaded, as Hungary had been three months before.

On June 5, an apprehensive General Guisan called a meeting of his high command 'working committee': Huber, Gonard, Bracher and Masson. Masson wondered whether the whole thing might be an act of revenge engineered by Schellenberg, but he kept his thoughts to himself. It was now estimated, unofficially, that the German divisions in the area of 200 kilometres numbered thirty-five. What was the significance of these groupings?

Masson, supported by Gonard, was in favour of mobilisation of the whole country. Huber, however, did not think that the situation was comparable with that of May and June 1940. The Wehrmacht was then intact and victorious, which was hardly the case in June 1944. Colonel Barbey, who followed Guisan wherever he went, made the following revealing remarks in his wartime diary:

"June 5—Struck, during this meeting, by the fidelity with which the Chief [General Guisan] sticks to his idea of a general mobilisation. Struck too by what was *not* said: no one, not even Masson, explained why the *Viking Line*, which until then had been so productive, could not be of any use in these circumstances. . . ."

The reason, of course, was obvious. Brigadier Masson could hardly let the whole world know that to save Switzerland he had been forced to incarcerate the head of this unique information network.

The next day, June 6, 1944, all Switzerland's fears disappeared. The Allies had landed in Normandy. At Bois-Mermet the detainees spent their days quietly. They had all been brought to the same prison—Roessler, Schneider, Duebendorfer, Foote, Hamel and Bolli—and put in separate comfortable cells. On September 8, 1944, when they were completely out of danger, they were released.

On his return to Wesemlin, where he found that nothing had been disturbed, not even his transmitter, Rudolf Roessler wasted no time in sending out a call to his ten friends in the OKW. He was fearful for their safety. While in prison he had had all the newspapers at his disposal and had followed closely the details of the July 20 attempt on Hitler's life and the savage reprisals taken against the Wehrmacht High Command. What, he wondered, had happened to *Werther* and *Olga* in all the turmoil? He stayed all night at his set, listening. No answer came. Every day he repeated the attempt.

Finally, on September 15, he received a reply. They were happy to know that he was safe and free. They had come through the July tumult unscathed. Ten times they had slipped through the net of purges, unsuspected of having anything to do with the plot. Better still, when Heinz Guderian was appointed chief of staff of the Oberkommando of the Wehrmacht on July 21, 1944, he sacked all his colleagues, except one, their friend G. *Werther* could therefore continue its work. The Nazi beast was dying, but it was not yet dead.

From September 16, Rudolf Roessler began visiting his Swiss colleagues in the Bureau Ha once again. Unfortunately, his extremely valuable dispatches remained, unused, in a safe together with the copies of the others which had bled Germany to death. Who could they be given to? And why? In any case, the fate of Nazism was sealed. Its days were numbered.

For Switzerland, the war was already over. It had ended on September 5, 1944, when General de Lattre de Tassigny's Moroccan troops marched along its frontiers on their way to Germany. From that date, the Confederation lifted its black-out regulations. It was already making preparations for its peace celebrations.

After a long stay in a Lausanne hotel, Alexander Foote decided to try and get in touch with his colleagues. After careful searching, he found Rachel Duebendorfer at the end of November, thanks to Pierre Nicole, the son of the Swiss Communist leader. From her, Foote learnt that Rado, who had remained in hiding in Berne, had left for Paris in order to renew contact with the Russians, who had already opened an embassy there.

"What are you going to do?" she asked.

"Go and join him."

"Then, before you go, you must see 'Lucy'. He will give you some documents for the Russians."

A meeting was arranged for December 15, at the Bolognese restaurant, in the Kazernenstrasse in Zürich. Foote arrived first, with 'Sissi'. At exactly mid-day, he saw a smallish man winding his way among the tables towards them. An unobtrusive man in his fifties, with an emaciated face and feverish eyes blinking behind spectacles. At first sight a colourless enough figure, but Foote was fascinated by the subtle impression of power he emanated. Roessler nibbled at his food without interest, but he talked a great deal—in a quick, nervous, rather jerky way. He talked of the war and of the Nazism that must be purged from the whole of Germany. He handed Foote a bulging brief-case:

"Sissi tells me you're leaving for Paris. I want you to do something for me. Here are the latest plans of the Wehrmacht. Give them to the Russians. Tell them to work out a system which will enable me to continue to send them all the information I receive from Germany. My network was not affected by the purges that followed July 20. This Germany must be crushed once and for all."

As they were leaving the restaurant, Roessler repeated his request for a means of corresponding with Moscow.

"Do you think it is still worth it?" Foote asked.

"I don't see what you mean," Roessler answered.

"Well," Foote explained, "as things are at the moment, the war can't go on much longer. I have a feeling that the 'Centre' no longer needs us, because the Red Army no longer needs the 'Centre'. Our work is finished, 'Lucy', and we've got to realise it. I'll take these documents to Paris, but I think I know what they'll say. They'll say that it's all over!"

A sudden transformation seemed to come over Rudolf Roessler. He seemed to have aged. Without a word of good-bye to either 'Sissi' or Alexander Foote, he turned on his heel and walked off, muttering incredulously to himself: "All over?"

Conclusion

VERY OFTEN THE EXISTENCE of people who are revealed to the public by some dramatic event seems to end with the event itself. Yet those people are human beings like the rest of us. They go on living, though usually deeply affected, sometimes even traumatised by the events they have experienced.

It is inconceivable that Roessler, Schellenberg, Masson, Foote and the others could have lived through that second world conflict without being profoundly affected by the terrible events they had witnessed.

From 1914 to 1918, 8,700,000 men lost their lives: including 1,390,000 French, 1,950,000 Germans, 1,000,000 Austrians and Hungarians, 780,000 British, 120,000 Americans and 1,700,000 Russians.

Between 1939 and 1945, more than 36,000,000 people were killed, including 6,000,000 Germans, 2,000,000 Japanese, 5,800,000 Poles, 1,600,000 Yugoslavs, 570,000 French, 400,000 British, 400,000 Americans—and 17,000,000 Russians.

It seemed only right, therefore, that this book should not end as abruptly as the activities of the 'Lucy' ring. So we pursued our investigations beyond the end of the Second World War in order to discover what had become of the leading actors in the extraordinary drama. Some of them seem to have vanished without trace—returning to the shadow world from which they came. Others, like Rachel Duebendorfer and Paul Boetcher, set off for the USSR in 1945. They no sooner arrived than they were quietly removed to work camps in Siberia. They remained there for twelve years—until they were released under Krushchev's liberalising measures. Stalin wanted to rid himself of any witnesses who might tarnish his reputation as a strategist of genius—by revealing to the Russians, for example, that German resisters had helped them defeat Hitler.

Rudolf Roessler did not leave Switzerland in 1945. He continued to work in his publishing house, the Vita Nova Verlag, in Lucerne and continued to live in his modest house at Wesemlin. He still had his transmitter-receiver, but it lay unused and useless, because there was no longer anyone at the other end, either the Russians or *Werther* and *Olga*. As Foote had led him to understand, the Russians no longer needed him, even when, after the war, he went to their fine new embassy in Berne and offered his services. Roessler found it even more inconceivable that when the war was over his friends in the former OKW left him without news—no messages, no letters, no visits, nothing but silence. It was inexplicable. Later, Roessler and his wife Olga together worked out a psychological hypothesis.

In their desire to stamp out Nazism from Germany, his ten companions had not realised that the death of the Third Reich would bring about the death of Germany. They would never be able to return to the pre-1933 Germany they had loved. They realised this only when they saw the Red Army in Berlin and the division of their country into two blocs which followed. Seeing at last the full results of their actions —a permanent resistance operated since 1939—they took the terrible decision not to meet again, to ignore each other's existence.

If this had indeed been his friends' state of mind, it was

certainly not Roessler's. He had no regrets. What he had done he had done in full consciousness of the outcome. He knew that if Nazism had triumphed, the world would have known considerably more than thirty-six million dead—not to mention the dark night into which it would have been plunged.

Roessler also realised that the end of Hitler and the defeat of Germany did not mean that all the Nazis had been got rid of. Many, who were lying low, would emerge later. Some had escaped their just deserts, while others, like the mysterious Gehlen, had 'changed sides' and were working for the western Allies until they could come out in their true colours. No, Foote had been wrong when he had said that it was 'all over'. His ten friends might have retired into their ivory towers, but he would not give up.

So when in the spring of 1947, an officer in civilian dress, Captain Wolf, of the Czech legation in Switzerland, called on Rudolf Roessler at his office in the Vita Nova Verlag and asked him to draw up analyses of the military and strategic situation in Europe, he agreed, convinced that by doing so he would be continuing to work for peace.

In 1939, it was his friend Xavier Schnieper who had introduced him to active espionage work by introducing him to Major Hausamann, of the Bureau Ha. In turn, Roessler now called on Schnieper's services—a more and more Left-wing Schnieper. In 1945 he had become chief librarian of the canton of Lucerne. He then worked for the Caritas organisation, where he became literary director, and which involved frequent visits to Prague. Schnieper joined the Swiss socialist party and became a journalist on *Volksrecht*, which sent him to Bonn as its permanent correspondent. In fact, it was there that Schnieper became Roessler's agent. He also met the Czech Captain Wolf. When this officer returned home in 1951, Roessler and Schnieper corresponded with two other Czechs, of which they only knew the nicknames, 'Conrad 1' and 'Conrad 2'.

In January 1953, Roessler went to West Germany, to

Düsseldorf, to write a thirteen-page report on military power in Europe. This report was intended for Czechoslovakia. First, however, it had to be sent to Zürich, to an agent whose sole function was to receive the mail and dispatch it to its real destination.

The report did not contain any major secrets. It had been based on official publications circulating in NATO circles. However, Roessler thought fit to hide it—in a pot of honey —for postage. An 'anonymous person', who occupied a high post in West Germany and who had been following Roessler's activities for some time, alerted the Swiss police. The parcel was intercepted. In March 1953, Otto Maurer, a police officer of Lucerne, arrested Rudolf Roessler and Xavier Schnieper.

They were given two hundred and forty-two days of preventative detention before being brought to trial on Monday, November 2, 1953. This was the time it had taken for the Swiss police to build up their case—or to 'make up' their case, as some people suggested.

The trial lasted for three days. The Federal judge, Corrodi, presided over the penal tribunal of Lucerne, assisted by Judges Pometta, Rais, Albrecht and Schwarz. The prosecution was led by the assistant public prosecutor, Haenni. Roessler was defended by Schuerch, of Berne, and Schnieper by Eckert, of Basle.

What was the charge against these two men? They were accused of spying on the West German Federal Republic for Czechoslovakia—of sending one hundred and sixty reports to Prague, in exchange for 33,000 Swiss francs. The defence proved that these reports were based on publications that could be bought by anyone in any book-shop. Roessler was condemned to one year's imprisonment and Schnieper to nine months.

Rudolf Roessler realised that something had changed in the Confederation. This was no longer the Switzerland that had shown itself to be so accommodating towards his activities, that from 1939 had accepted the secrets of the OKW, that had allowed the transmission of so much information to the Soviet Union and which, in 1945, had presented him with an expression of its gratitude for his conduct during the war. Disillusioned, indifferent and exhausted, Rudolf Roessler died in October 1958. Few people attended his funeral at Kriens—his colleagues and Xavier Schnieper. None of his war-time comrades were there. He went, as spies always do, even the greatest of them, discreetly. A small marble plaque bears the simple statement:

"Rudolf Roessler. 1897-1958."

Xavier Schnieper still lives in Lucerne, where he works as a journalist and writer. He often meets Rudolf Roessler's former partners who still run the Vita Nova Verlag. But he rarely sees Major Hans Hausamann, now a photographer in Zürich, the former head of the Bureau Ha, to whom he introduced the German émigré in 1939.

In 1945, as the Third Reich was drawing to its agonised end, Walter Schellenberg arrived at the Swedish frontier with a party of Scandinavian internees whom he had freed from concentration camps for the occasion, with the agreement of Heinrich Himmler. The SS-Brigadeführer knew that one never arrives empty-handed when one wants something. What he wanted was asylum. Count Bernadotte agreed to let him stay temporarily in Stockholm.

Bernadotte also helped him to get to Britain. On June 16, 1945, a transport plane took him secretly to London. In exchange, he had promised to reveal everything he knew concerning matters that interested the British government. Such a proposition, coming from the head of the Sicherheitsdienst, who must have sensational information on the events that had taken place in the world since 1933 and on the men who had brought these events about, was too valuable to spurn.

For three years Schellenberg talked to satisfy the curiosity of the British agents. The result was an impressive harvest of information, though, of course, the experts of the Intelligence Service had to separate the wheat from the chaff. For Schellenberg often lied or twisted the truth to his own advantage. But the truth that emerged more than justified the time and energy spent on obtaining it.

On January 4, 1946, Schellenberg gave evidence against the Nazi leaders at Nuremberg. No one was surprised when Schellenberg returned to London, flanked by two nurses. He was a sick man—stones were forming in his bladder. Back in London he was given treatment. When he had fully recovered, the interrogation continued.

In 1948, squeezed dry of information by the British, he was placed at the mercy of the international court that was still in session in Nuremberg. Schellenberg appeared before the judges towards the end of spring 1949. His defence counsel would have had little difficulty in getting him acquitted—the British and Americans having given their agreement—if the Soviet delegate had not intervened strongly against such a decision. Naturally, the Russians found it incredible that the western Allies should want to acquit the former head of the Sicherheitsdienst. As a result Schellenberg was given four years.

In 1952, three years after his condemnation, the British had him released—on health grounds. He knew where to go. He got in touch with his old enemy, Roger Masson. Moved somewhat by Schellenberg's obvious physical and mental deterioration, Masson agreed to give him what help he could—secretly, for the Swiss might not take kindly to such help. He entrusted Schellenberg to one of his friends, a surgeon called Lang, who hid the German near Romont, half-way between Lausanne and Freiburg. After a few months' respite, the Federal authorities learnt of his presence there and ordered his immediate expulsion.

It was little more than a moribund Schellenberg who left for the shores of Lake Como—where he was supported by money from the British government. He began writing his memoirs—but they were finished by a professional, a German journalist. A number of people were relieved when these memoirs finally appeared to see that Schellenberg had, in fact, revealed very little. He died in the autumn of 1954.

One of the last living witnesses of this extraordinary

affair, Alexander Foote, also wrote a book—a small, consciously incomplete work, on the 'advice' no doubt of the British counter-espionage service. For Foote left the Communist Party and is now living respectably in Britain.

In December 1944, after his first and only meeting with Rudolf Roessler in the Bolognese in Zürich, Foote went to Paris, with the documents given him by 'Lucy'. This mass of information enabled him to be received at the Soviet embassy where, at first, he was thought to be an agent provocateur. The expert who examined the papers immediately got in touch with the 'Centre', which said that Foote was to go to Moscow. He was to travel with Alexander Rado, who had been in Paris for some weeks.

Rado and Foote celebrated their reunion with caviar and vodka. Under the effects of alcohol Rado lost some of his caution. He admitted he was frightened. First, because he had abandoned his post at a dangerous moment and, secondly, because he had never been able to distinguish between the money he had been sent for the running of his network and his own salary. He knew he had 'embezzled' something like 50,000 dollars. What could he do? If he went into hiding, he would be condemned just as surely as if he had admitted to working for the Nazis. If the MGB really wanted to rid itself of an agent, they would find him.

On January 6, 1945, at 9 a.m., the first Soviet plane to leave Paris since 1939 took off from Le Bourget. On board was a cargo of Russian officers and two civilians, Foote and Rado. The pilot was to make a vast détour. There was no point in exposing oneself to possible danger by flying over Germany—the war was not quite over yet. They would reach Moscow via Egypt and Turkey and break the journey for forty-eight hours in Cairo.

When the DC3 took off again at dawn on January 9, one of the civilian passengers was no longer there. Rado had disappeared into the Egyptian night.

On January 11, Foote was in Moscow. He was warmly welcomed. He was even given a charming female interpreter who would take care of him until he was called before a commission which would examine his conduct during the war. He had no difficulty in showing that he had been unable to escape arrest in November 1943, which had deprived the Red Army of 'Lucy's' valuable information.

He was questioned for a long time about 'Lucy' and about the functioning of the network. Then, freed from any trace of suspicion, he was sent to the famous spy school at Sekhjodnya—after which, no doubt, he would be ready once more to serve. He proved a brilliant pupil and was even given the rank of major of the Red Army, which brought with it a more than adequate salary. In the course of the summer of 1945, he learnt by chance at Sekhjodnya that Rado had finally been extradited from Cairo, where he was found by agents of the MGB, judged and summarily executed.

The news of the treatment meted out to the former head of his network, which was proof enough that one could never trifle with the 'Centre', did nothing to deepen Foote's conviction that communism was still the best possible social system at man's disposal. Gradually, as his experience as a secret agent grew, he began to lose his illusions. So when at the beginning of March 1947, his masters considered he was ready to confront the capitalist world once more and he was flown to East Berlin, he decided that he would get out at the first good opportunity. He had a new identity— that of Albert Mueller, a German. At the end of July, he learnt that he would be sent to Mexico, where he was to work as the resident-director of a network, spying on the United States.

The time had come, he thought, to change sides. On August 2, 1947, he escaped and presented himself to the authorities of the British sector in Berlin.

Today Alexander Foote works for the British government. But he might never have gone back to Britain had he known that Alexander Rado was not dead, but that he had only been told so as a warning. Rado is now professor of geography at the University of Budapest, old but still useful despite twelve years spent, like Rachel Duebendorfer, in a Siberian work-camp.

And what of the other characters in this drama? Many of them are dead, like General Guisan, who was accompanied to the Pully cemetery, in Lausanne, on April 12, 1960, by more than 200,000 Swiss soldiers who had come down spontaneously from their mountains to pay their last respects to the man who had realised that 'total neutrality' would not have saved the Confederation between 1939 and 1945, and who had preferred an 'active neutrality'.

But one of the most tormented actors in this tragedy was Roger Masson.

Long ago, France could have given him the Legion of Honour, Britain its Distinguished Service Order, America its Distinguished Service Cross, and the Soviet Union its Red Star. Like Guisan, he too served the Allies' cause—in the interests of Switzerland. One might even be permitted to wonder why post-war Switzerland, which condemned Rudolf Roessler to prison, did not also deal with its former secret service chief.

As Walter Schellenberg had foreseen when he planned his diabolical scheme to force Roger Masson to visit him in September 1942, it was the brigadier who had to take the blame when, after the war, the facts became known. It happened in a particularly cruel way.

On September 28, 1945, the Swiss press announced that on the 21st of the same month, Roger Masson, in an interview with the *Chicago Daily News*, had disclosed that during the war he had met Walter Schellenberg, the head of the Sicherheitsdienst, on several occasions—the first time in Germany, then subsequently in Switzerland.

Two Federal deputies, Herr Dietchi, a Radical from Basle, and Herr Bringolf, a Socialist from Schaffhouse, immediately went into attack. They expressed astonishment that such contacts could have taken place, inferred that the head of the Swiss secret service had been duped by Schellenberg, and declared that in any case Masson had considerably exceeded the brief that had been entrusted to him. They demanded that an inquiry into the whole 'affair' be opened at once.

They had their way. Judge Couchepin opened a government inquiry on October 23, 1945. On January 28, 1946, he published his conclusions: the brigadier was entirely exonerated of any suspicion.

Entirely? Such attacks always leave their scars. Even today, there are pro-Masson and anti-Masson parties in Switzerland. Roger Masson never really recovered from the accusations made against him—because he has never been able to tell the truth. He has been unable to defend himself in broad daylight, because of the oath of secrecy which prevents him from revealing the slightest details about this still recent, still controversial period. His military career was cut short on September 28, 1945. From that, too, he has never recovered.

We met him several times in the Hôtel de Lausanne, in the centre of that city. Masson feels at home there. When he was head of the Swiss secret service he often used this large, somewhat anonymous hotel for appointments; with its numerous exits and its proximity to the station, it was particularly suitable for meetings which should remain unnoticed. Today, twenty years later, with no longer any particular reason for doing so, it was there that he arranged to meet us.

He received us cordially. He talked of his meetings with Schellenberg. But when, one day, we asked him certain embarrassing questions concerning Rudolf Roessler, Brigadier Masson rose to his feet, looked straight at us and, without a word, walked away. We did not see him again.

The day before, he had said to us: "A few days ago it was my seventieth birthday. I spent it quietly at home on Mont-Pèlerin, the hill overlooking Vevey. To my great surprise, the postman arrived that morning with hundreds of letters. Hundreds of men had remembered—former colleagues of mine. It was my best birthday for twenty years."

And what about Switzerland itself? After all, it formed

the background to this extraordinary participation in history. Was it, too, marked by events?

The Swiss do not like it to be said, but the Confederation did not suffer from the war.

Switzerland was bombed on a few occasions, accidentally: Burgen in October 1941, Basle and Zürich in December of the same year. These were mistakes committed by the RAF. There were a small number of victims. In autumn 1944, the American air force also made mistakes. They bombed the railway-station at Delémont, the Soleure-Moutier train and the Basle-Zürich express, near Pratteln. Mougins was bombed. On February 22, 1945, eleven raids on Stein-am-Rhein and Ruf killed eighteen Swiss and wounded fifty. On March 4, it was Zürich's turn. These were all the result of aerial attacks on objectives situated near the frontier—their calculations a few kilometres out.

Contrary to what has sometimes been claimed, Switzerland was never seriously short of food—far from it. The most it ever suffered was a temporary, and never very severe rationing of some food-stuffs.

During the war Switzerland performed a number of actions that conformed to its popular image. Parcels sent from the Confederation did much to alleviate the distress of prisoners of war. Between November 1940 and December 1942, Switzerland gave a three-months' holiday to 21,365 children from France, Belgium and Yugoslavia.

But one cannot forget that the same Switzerland turned away thousands of Jewish children, who ended their lives in gas-chambers. "We took in a hundred thousand of them," it is often said.

It should be explained that out of the 100,000 refugees accepted by the Confederation between 1933 and 1945, there were exactly 21,944 Jews. To conclude this painful chapter in its history, we feel we cannot do better than borrow the words of the Dutch government. In 1952, in a report on the attitude of Switzerland towards the Netherlands, they wrote:

"We should both thank Switzerland and refrain from doing so. . . ."

It should not be forgotten either that Switzerland gave invaluable help to the enemies of Nazism. Was the rôle of Switzerland an indispensable one in the defeat of Hitler?

If it is true that the secret services contribute more to victory on the battle-field than do the generals then, without doubt, Switzerland had a rightful share in the victory of 1945. Without Switzerland and the hospitality her government gave to the most fantastic anti-Nazi resistance-network, the war might well have ended differently.

This affair was undoubtedly responsible also for the final collapse of the myth of Swiss neutrality. In its place a new image of the Confederation emerged, that of a country sharing, like every other country, in the glory and horror of the world's great upheavals.

Contrary to what has often been said, history has not deserted Switzerland.